A MOVEMENT
OF THE PEOPLE

Frontispiece. From its very beginning the AEQA had a dedicated staff led throughout its existence by AEQA founders Martha McInnis (center, front) and John Bloomer (right). As its programs and efforts expanded, so did the AEQA staff, which by the late 1970s and early 1980s included (from left) Barbara Ware, Donnie Butler, Mike Schrier, Gillis Morgan, Dana Kerbs Urrutia, and Dot Drablos. (Courtesy of the AEQA.)

A MOVEMENT OF THE PEOPLE

The Roots of Environmental Education and Advocacy in Alabama

KATIE LAMAR JACKSON

FOREWORD BY DAVID MATHEWS

THE UNIVERSITY OF ALABAMA PRESS

Tuscaloosa

The University of Alabama Press
Tuscaloosa, Alabama 35487-0380
uapress.ua.edu

Typeface: Minion and Futura Condensed

Cover image: A one-mile walking trail in Tuskegee National Forest that
was part of William Bartram's route through Alabama became the first
designated US Forest Service Trail in the nation. Pictured (from left) at
the trail's dedication are AEQA Executive Vice President Martha McInnis;
Tuskegee Mayor Johnny Ford; G. J. Koellsted, manager of the Auburn
University Theatre who depicted Bartram during the event; Congressman
Bill Nichols, who was instrumental in achieving the trail designation; an
unidentified member of the Prattville YMCA "Indian dancers" troop that
gave a presentation at the event; and Arthur Woody, state Forest Service
supervisor with the US Department of Agriculture. Courtesy of AEQA.
Cover design: Mary-Frances Burt / Burt & Burt

Library of Congress Cataloging-in-Publication Data

Names: Jackson, Katie Lamar. author.
Title: A movement of the people : the roots of environmental education and
advocacy in Alabama / Katie Lamar Jackson ; foreword by David Mathews.
Description: Tuscaloosa : The University of Alabama Press, [2017] |
Includes index.
Identifiers: LCCN 2017004050| ISBN 9780817359027 (pbk.) |
ISBN 9780817391522 (e book)
Subjects: LCSH: Alabama Environmental Quality Association. |
Environmentalism—Alabama—History—20th century. | Environmental
education—Alabama—History—20th century. | Women and the
environment—Alabama—History.
Classification: LCC GE185.A2 J33 2017 | DDC 304.209761—dc23
LC record available at https://lccn.loc.gov/2017004050

Contents

Figures

Foreword

This book comes at a time when many Americans doubt they can make a significant difference in our political system and government. They want to; they are just not sure how. Although the subject here is the Alabama Environmental Quality Association (AEQA), the book is about much more than that. It is a case study focusing on what everyday citizens can accomplish by joining forces. It is a story of the power of the associations and networks citizens can build.

The heroine of this story is Martha McInnis, whom I met in the 1970s when I was president of the University of Alabama. College students, then and now, tend to be very idealistic; they want change. I thought Alabamians like Martha were the best teachers these young people could have because she was making a difference. We became good friends, and I am honored to be asked to write this foreword.

The dominant theory of change is that it comes about as the result of leadership from prestigious people, the influence of large institutions like corporations and governments, and money, lots of money. There is no doubt that these elements are powerful. Yet Martha's hero, Lance Tompkins, who laid the foundation for the AEQA with his anti-litter initiative, was a rural mail carrier.

Rural mail carriers don't fit into the prevailing theory of how change is made. And Lance did not act alone; he was only one of the many Alabamians who were part of the state's environmental movement. People just like Lance, and others who were more notable, formed a vast statewide environmental network of people and organizations "with divergent social and political leanings." For me, this networking is the real story because it shows that people do not have to fully agree to work together effectively. Differences are not a barrier unless we let them be so. The people who created the movement made a profound discovery: they realized that they did not have to like one another; they just had to recognize that they needed one another. We do not know the names of all the Lance Tompkins in the Alabama environmental movement, but we should not forget the importance of hundreds—perhaps even thousands—of nameless acts by hundreds or even thousands of nameless people who did—and still do—what they can to keep Alabama beautiful. No effort, however small, is insignificant when joined with similar efforts.

Organizations come and go. That is the way of the world. But ideals and hopes live on. That's the AEQA's legacy, despite the association's untimely death in 1983. The loss of state funding ended the formal organization; still, that was not the only resource the movement had. Its members had civic assets, which do not have to be appropriated by legislatures, although they do have to be recognized by citizens and communities. The assets are so ordinary that they tend to be overlooked. They include the experiences of people and their sense of what is valuable to the state. These are put to use when citizens have to exercise their faculty for judging what is the right thing to do about a problem or policy issue, which is often the case when environmental concerns have to be balanced with economic imperatives. This faculty, along with the array of skills people have, is magnified when citizens make use of their ability to connect, collaborate, and form alliances across social, political, and economic divides.

Even though the AEQA closed its doors years ago, environmental initiatives still open other doors every day across Alabama. The association did not die in vain; its spirit is reborn every time a new Lance Tompkins appears on the scene or a new Martha McInnis begins to get neighbors working with neighbors. Those Alabamians revitalize both our natural and our political ecosystems.

David Mathews

President and CEO, Kettering Foundation, Dayton, Ohio

Former President of the University of Alabama,

1969–75 and 1977–80

Preface

Sometimes history takes us places we have never been. Sometimes it takes us back to times and places we have long forgotten. Sometimes it does both.

That is what I discovered when, in the fall of 2013, I began working with Martha McInnis to chronicle the history of the Alabama Environmental Quality Association (AEQA), a once powerful but now virtually forgotten environmental education organization that existed in Alabama from the late 1960s through the early 1980s.

I was "introduced" to the AEQA when Martha, who helped found and lead the AEQA throughout its existence, contacted me about writing a history of the organization. At that point I knew nothing of the organization despite the fact that I came of age in its heyday. However, I was soon to learn that, though the organization had no place in my memory, much of its story was tied to my own past.

Among those ties is the AEQA's origin within the Alabama Farm

Bureau Federation (now the Alabama Farmers Federation and Alfa Insurance), an organization that I was involved in through its Young Farmers program in the early and mid-1980s and then as its director of publications from 1987 to 1988. I not only had never heard of the AEQA during my Farm Bureau years, I was more than a little surprised to learn that any environmental organization had roots there.

What ultimately intrigued me about the AEQA and made me want to write this book, however, was its role in Alabama's social and political history. The AEQA story is a tale about the power (and often empowerment) of women, minorities, and others in rural and urban communities who came together to form a grassroots movement that adroitly navigated a conservative southern political system to reach and teach fellow citizens. It is also a story about the environmental concerns—strip mining, climate change, hazardous and solid waste disposal, wetland and wilderness conservation, energy conservation, water quality protection, historical preservation, and recycling among them—that our state faced nearly five decades ago and continues to face today.

In researching this book, I relied heavily on Martha's recollections of the AEQA (stories told in Martha's distinctive Montgomery inflections, the gentleness of which belies her tenacity and grit) as well as the memories of others who were involved with the organization. Martha also provided me with a waist-high stack of oversized, meticulously compiled and curated AEQA scrapbooks that were invaluable in the writing of this book and in my own education—re-education, really—about Alabama's environmental history.

Sitting cross-legged for hours on my office floor, I pored through the news clippings, photos, and letters within those scrapbooks and realized that I *did* know about the AEQA, or at least about its programs. As a preteen and teenager, I had actually participated in some of those programs, such as recycling and cleanup efforts, without ever knowing that the AEQA was behind them.

Those scrapbooks also offered me a remarkably candid view of the AEQA and its time and place in Alabama history. Their pages were covered with photos and news clipping featuring not just state and national leaders who were involved with the AEQA but also everyday citizens who were the life blood of AEQA's community programs. There were also stories and editorials that addressed the history of the state's environmental efforts, brought the era to life on page after page, and chronicled not only the AEQA's successes but also its challenges.

One of the AEQA's greatest resources, its political connections, was also its greatest hindrance. Its close ties to Farm Bureau and to then-Governor George Wallace, which the AEQA was quite adroit at leveraging, raised more than a few eyebrows and sometimes the ire of environmentalists and others in the state who felt the AEQA's cozy relationship with these powerful people and entities was at odds with the goals of environmental activism.

The truth is, the AEQA did not focus on activism. It passionately took on education as its mission. And it was not shy about navigating the political system to further that mission, a choice that eventually led to its demise but that also allowed the AEQA to work within the system to create some exceptional programs, the effects of which are still felt and seen in our state.

Those effects may well have implications for today's environmental movements. Certainly, lessons learned from the AEQA's successes and failures have value for modern environmentalists—what to do and what not to do. But perhaps more importantly, the telling of this story can lead to some of the programs and projects instituted by the AEQA being salvaged as models and templates for current and future environmental education movements.

My hope is that, by recounting the story of the AEQA, we fill in a missing gap in Alabama's environmental history, affording us all a chance to learn things we did not know as well as rediscover things we had forgotten and, most important of all, use that knowledge to make sure we live up to the moniker "Alabama the Beautiful."

Acknowledgments

Writing a history of a bygone organization the likes of the Alabama Environmental Quality Association (AEQA), an institution that shut its doors more than four decades ago and has been long out of the public eye, could have been a daunting endeavor. But it was not, and that is because I had access to so many people and archival resources that it was an embarrassment of riches for which I am very grateful.

I am first and foremost grateful to Martha McInnis, the woman who was the life force of the AEQA for some sixteen years and whose deft memories of those years brought this book to life. I thank her for walking me through this history and for trusting me to tell it.

I am also deeply grateful to Nancy Callahan, Carolyn Dunlavy, Frank Filgo, Mike Forster, Mike Schrier, Hazel Mobley, Albert Brewer, Gillis Morgan, and Larry Martin for so generously sharing their memories with me. They have given this book depth, context, and dimension.

I am indebted, too, to the meticulous records that Martha and her staff kept through the years. These sources yielded a wealth of information not only about the AEQA but also about the times in which it operated. Research for this book relied heavily on this archival information, some of which was found in files at the Alabama Department of Archives and History, but much of which was found in the pages of old AEQA scrapbooks.

Within those scrapbook pages were letters, press releases, brochures, pamphlets, photographs, and newspaper and magazine clippings dating from 1967 to 1983. The sources for verbatim excerpts from newspapers and magazines found in those archives are cited in the text; however, more general information was also gleaned from a variety of newspaper and print publications such as the *Birmingham News/Post Herald*, *Montgomery Advertiser*, *Alabama Journal*, *Decatur Daily*, *Mobile Press/Register*, and *Farm Bureau News*.

A huge thank you goes to David Mathews, president and CEO of the Kettering Foundation, who graciously agreed to write the foreword to this book and then presented us with an eloquent, insightful piece of writing that so beautifully captures the subject's essence and importance.

My very deep appreciation also goes to Beth Motherwell, senior acquisitions editor for the natural sciences with the University of Alabama Press, who shepherded me through the publishing process. Her professional, thoughtful, and sensible guidance was vital and inestimable.

Special thanks also go to Ed Williams and John Carvalho of the Auburn University School of Communications and Journalism for putting Martha in touch with me so that we could even begin working on this book.

Martha and I both also thank our families, who have supported us individually in life and collectively in the writing of this book. I especially want to thank my husband, Kevin, who has tolerated the towering stacks of scrapbooks and other research material that have become part of our décor.

And last but not least, we salute the generations of women, men, and children who have worked to keep their communities clean and safe—the grassroots environmentalists who helped make the AEQA happen and continue to care for and protect Alabama's environment today and into the future.

Introduction

The history of environmental movements is long and complicated, a story of successes and failures that has often been driven by grassroots, bottom-up, citizen-driven action at its finest. Sometimes the organizers of such movements are fiery crusaders. At other times they are cool pragmatists. But regardless of the differences in style, they all share an intense, ardent desire to protect and preserve the natural world, and they do not hesitate to voice their concerns to their fellow citizens, particularly people in the position to effect change.

Such was the case when, in the mid-1960s, Lance Tompkins, a rural mail carrier from Dale County, Alabama, began trying to change the world he saw each day along his mail route. It was a world blemished by roadside rubbish piles and litter; he wanted to clean it up, restoring the beauty of his beloved Wiregrass region. So he took action by going to a powerful political entity in his state—the Alabama Farm Bureau Federation—and asking its leaders to address the issue by adding a rural cleanup request to their annual policy statements.

Tompkins probably did not think of himself as an activist or imagine that his policy request would ultimately bring together an unlikely coalition of farmers, rural and urban residents, the press, politicians, governmental agencies, civic groups, and many others with divergent social, economic, and political agendas to address the problem. But it did just that, as Tompkins's simple request sparked a movement that grew into the Alabama Environmental Quality Association (AEQA), an organization that during its existence taught thousands of people in Alabama and beyond how to preserve and protect their state's natural, cultural, and historical resources.

The story of the extraordinary movement that Tompkins instigated spans three decades, during which time Alabama and the entire nation made both remarkable advances and vexing regressions in the areas of environmental protection and conservation. It is a story about grassroots activism and the ability of citizens—both the powerful and the previously un-empowered—to elicit much-needed progress. It is also an account of how leadership and politics can both enable and derail that progress, a long-standing and still-persistent problem in Alabama.

This book chronicles the history of the AEQA as it developed, evolved, and eventually dissolved, all in the midst of the climate of political and social upheaval and change that pervaded both the state and the nation at the time. It is not a story with a storybook ending, but perhaps more an Aesop's Fable for modern times—a tale both of how choices made do not always lead to the best outcome and of how there are valuable lessons to be learned from mistakes. But that makes it all the more important a story to tell as a reminder of Alabama's environmental history, as a lesson in organizing a grassroots movement, as a guide to sustaining that grassroots effort across generations, and perhaps even as a catalyst for reclaiming some of those past accomplishments and making future advances.

A MOVEMENT
OF THE PEOPLE

1

An Accidental Advocacy

There is nothing like riding the back roads of Alabama—the back roads of any state for that matter—to get a picture of a community and of human society that is sometimes distressing.

It was on just such back roads in Dale County during the 1960s that rural mail carrier Lance Tompkins saw both the beauty of his Wiregrass region of Alabama and the ugliness of society's residue. Trash littered the shoulders of the roads and piles of cast-off junk— from household garbage to the shells of derelict cars and rusted washing machines—were heaped indiscriminately along tree lines, fencerows, and in gullies, perhaps because local residents had no better place to dispose of these items or perhaps because they were unaware of the safety and health dangers posed by their discarded waste.

After years of seeing this environmental degradation, Tompkins decided to take action against the above eyesores and health hazards. He took his concerns to Montgomery, not to the Statehouse,

Figure 1. Roadside dumps filled with old tires and discarded herbicide cans were a common sight in Alabama when, in 1965, rural mail carrier Lance Tompkins went to the Alabama Farm Bureau Federation asking for a statewide rural cleanup campaign policy. These dumps were more than unsightly: they posed environmental and health threats to local residents. (Courtesy of the AEQA.)

but to what was then (and still is) one of the most powerful political entities in the state—the Alabama Farm Bureau Federation (AFB).

Each year the AFB developed policy statements addressing a host of issues, ranging from the organization's internal governance to statewide agricultural matters and political action agendas. Topics for those policies were often suggested by AFB members, and so it was that in 1965, Tompkins, as a member of the Dale County Farm Bureau Federation, proposed that the AFB's state leaders develop a policy encouraging the cleanup of the unsightly and unsanitary roadside dumps and litter that he encountered each day in his appointed rounds.

Tompkins's policy suggestion was, indeed, included in the Rural

Figure 2. Abandoned cars such as this were prevalent
along rural Alabama roads and byways, as were discarded
refrigerators and other appliances. These derelict eyesores often leaked chemicals such as oil, gas, and coolants; provided
a refuge for rats, snakes, and other vermin; and became
breeding grounds for mosquitos. In addition, such items
posed a threat of injury or entrapment to local residents,
particularly children. (Courtesy of the AEQA.)

Living section of *Farm Bureau Policies for 1967* and was officially adopted at the AFB's annual meeting held November 13–16, 1966, in Mobile, Alabama. It read:

> Rural Clean-Up Week
> We recommend that Farm Bureau, through its state organization, appeal to our Governor to promote a state-wide week (to include every residential community) in November of each year, whereby accumulated debris of a busy year might be disposed of, enhancing the appearance of homes, farms, and business establishments.
> This should be accomplished by an appeal by the Governor to all news media—radio, television, newspapers, etc.— to urge and support this needed clean-up.
> The purpose of this appeal is to make Alabama more attractive to both the traveling public and home residents.

Having established this new cleanup policy, the AFB Board of Directors implemented the idea by delegating it to a relatively new group within the organization—the AFB state Women's Committee (now known as the Alabama Farm Bureau Federation Women's Leadership Committee).

Members of that committee included women from throughout rural Alabama who were hand-picked because of their proven track record of leadership and engagement in their communities and with organizations such as the Alabama Cooperative Extension Service (now the Cooperative Extension System). Many of these women, primarily the wives of the AFB's male leaders, had worked informally for years in their local communities as the Farm Bureau's foot soldiers and ambassadors and had strong working relationships with local officials, civic groups, and the news media. Recognizing that these women held great potential for the Farm Bureau's lobbying and public relations efforts, the AFB had formed a state Women's Committee in 1965, putting them to work in a more official capacity.

According to Dot Smith, who was chairwoman of the AFB's first county Women's Committee in Tuscaloosa and later went on to lead the rural cleanup effort in her region and further its cause across the state, members of the Women's Committee were extremely dedicated and hardworking. "They had to be dedicated to be there," she said. "And they were always ready to do something."

Soon after the committee was formed, the AFB hired a young woman as the Women's Committee director who was as passionate and dynamic as the committee's members. That young woman was Martha McInnis, an Alabama native who had grown up on her family's dairy farm on the outskirts of Montgomery but had gone out in the world to build a career in business and academia.

McInnis—who had earned her bachelor's and master's degrees in the Department of Clothing, Textiles, and Related Arts from the University of Alabama's School of Home Economics (now the College of Human and Environmental Sciences)—first left Alabama in 1962 to work on a temporary faculty appointment at the University of Miami. A year later, she went to work as the adult education consultant for McCall Corporation's Pattern Education Division in New York City.

In that capacity, McInnis traveled across the nation for McCall presenting lecture demonstrations about clothing and textiles to adult education, Cooperative Extension, and college and high school groups in major cities. She also conducted programs on commercial and educational television, directed workshops for home economics teachers in cooperation with retail stores, and developed visual aids for effective teaching.

While the McCall job was exciting and certainly taught McInnis a great deal about public speaking and negotiating the politics of business and people nationwide, she grew tired of a life of travel and the often unveiled resentment shown toward her as a white Southerner during those years of civil rights upheaval. When—in the fall of 1964—she got an offer to join the faculty at Arizona State University (ASU) in Tempe, Arizona, McInnis left the world of commerce and business to become an assistant professor.

The ASU position gave McInnis a new opportunity to stretch her wings creatively and intellectually. At the same time, while she loved her job, she also missed the South and her family, a longing that became greater after McInnis's father passed away and health problems landed her mother in the hospital. It was during that time that McInnis came home to Montgomery for a short visit and happened upon a local job announcement that looked appealing.

"I was sitting in my mother's room at Baptist Hospital in June of 1966 entertaining myself by reading the want ads," McInnis recalled. She noticed an ad for a position at the Alabama Farm Bureau Insurance Company, the offices of which were just across the street from the hospital.

"I walked across the street and left a resume with Dick McGowan, senior vice president of personnel for the insurance company," she said. McGowan knew that the advertised job was not a good fit for McInnis, but he asked to keep her resume saying that the Federation (the agricultural arm of Farm Bureau's insurance company) was undergoing an expansion and might have an opening in the future. Approximately seven months later McInnis got a call from the AFB asking if she would be interested in a new Women's Program Coordinator position to help lead the Women's Committee's activities and development.

Martha was intrigued by the job description. It was an opportunity to build the nascent women's program and be back home, but when she interviewed and discovered that she would be involved in lobbying the Alabama Legislature and the US Congress, she became especially interested in the position. "I always loved politics," said Martha, noting that, had circumstances for women been different in that era, she might well have pursued a career in law and politics rather than fashion design.

Still, taking the job required her to do some soul searching. "I fully intended to get my PhD, but it's funny how life takes a lot of directions and you don't know where paths will lead you," she said. Ultimately, it was encouragement from Louise Cockrell—another nationally known woman in the world of academia with whom McInnis worked at ASU—and her husband, a Beverly Hills banker, that convinced McInnis to say "yes" to the job offer. "They said, 'The Sunbelt is growing and, with you being from the South and wanting to go home, maybe your opportunity is in the South,'" said McInnis.

McInnis joined the Farm Bureau staff in February 1967 and set to work helping guide the then–two-year-old committee. Her initial task was to strengthen the committee's structure and establish new networks for its programs and activities, with particular focus on helping solve local rural issues. She soon realized that this was a group of women who were already well versed in political action. "I don't know if the Farm Bureau men realized these women had political savvy, but they did recognize that they would be useful," said McInnis of the nascent committee. "The bottom line was that, when the leadership of the Farm Bureau wanted to get out the vote, that's how those men got things done—through the women."

With McInnis's help, the committee began to broaden its network of county committees and expand its work on such projects as a door-to-door membership campaign aimed at recruiting one hundred thousand members and establishing the Political Education and Action Program (PEP). Of all its accomplishments, however, McInnis cites work with rural cleanup issues as one of the committee's greatest, a project that was given to it as something of an afterthought.

Figure 3. Because many residents, both rural and urban, had no access to sanitary landfills or garbage services, unofficial dumping sites often sprang up throughout communities, where residents discarded everything from household garbage to dead animals. (Courtesy of the AEQA.)

Environmental action and advocacy were probably not on Mc-Innis's or the committee members' radar screens at the time, but once the idea of a statewide rural cleanup campaign had been sponsored and endorsed by the AFB, the state board handed it off to the women-folk saying, "Come up with something so we can say we've done something," recalled McInnis.

The women ran with it. Took off with it, in fact.

"Those women did a lot, but that cleanup campaign to me was one of the committee's longest-lasting contributions, not only to agriculture but to the entire state," said McInnis. "Today, Alabama has a sanitary landfill law that requires county governing bodies to provide a garbage collection disposal system. That's because of Farm Bureau women!"

2

A Suggestion Becomes a Movement

"I didn't know too much about what could be done," admitted McInnis
of the rural cleanup project that had been handed to her and her
committee. Still, since she subscribed to a "no such thing as can't"
philosophy (something she had learned from her former University
of Alabama professor and mentor Henrietta Thompson), McInnis
set to work.

One of her first contacts was A. W. Jones, a retired economist in
Auburn University's School of Agriculture (now College of Agriculture) who was at the time serving as an AFB consultant.

"Mr. Jones was very quiet, but very perceptive," recalled McInnis.
"He would make a statement and smile pleasantly, but he could always see the possibilities of a situation." McInnis developed a friend-
ship with Jones during his frequent visits to the AFB building, and
he, recognizing the potential of the rural cleanup campaign, was
eager to help.

At the time, Jones wrote a weekly column for the *Birmingham
News* (he later became the *News*'s farm editor), and he volunteered

to introduce McInnis to John Bloomer, then the paper's managing editor. According to McInnis, "Mr. Jones greatly admired John Bloomer's ability to recognize good news and, with a twinkle in his eye, said this was something Bloomer would be interested in."

Bloomer, a native of Indiana who had come to the South in the 1930s as a young journalist working for papers in Tennessee, Florida, Virginia, Mississippi, and Georgia, understood well the power of the pen and never hesitated to use that clout to promote social change. He had joined the *Birmingham News* staff in 1959 as an editorial writer, having come to the *News* from the *Columbus Ledger* and *Sunday Ledger-Enquirer* sister papers in Georgia where he had served as managing editor. During his tenure there, the papers were awarded the 1955 Pulitzer Prize for Public Service for their coverage of the Phenix City corruption and crime cleanup. Once McInnis told him about the rural cleanup campaign, Bloomer soon found himself involved with another cleanup story—this time the tidying up of Alabama's environment.

According to McInnis, Bloomer listened intently as she laid out the program for a Rural Cleanup Week that had, at the AFB's urging, been proclaimed for November 27 through December 1, 1967, by then–Alabama Governor Lurleen Wallace. The journalist was interested in the project in part because he was civic-minded, said McInnis, but also because he saw it as a way to both mend fences and harness the potential of the AFB.

The previous year, *News* writer Ted Pearson had penned an in-depth investigative article critical of the Farm Bureau's insurance company, which had, quite naturally, drawn the ire of AFB leadership. Bloomer recognized that the Rural Cleanup project was an opportunity to rebuild a relationship with the Farm Bureau; it was also a chance for the *News* to spur the AFB and other groups into further action on the environmental front.

"As our meeting drew to a close, Mr. Bloomer asked if I could provide the *News* with a week's worth of county cleanup features and photo possibilities," recalled McInnis. "If so, he would feature a story each day for a week in the paper. I had no idea whether we could line up these stories, but the offer was too good to turn down." Sure enough, McInnis helped find the stories, and Bloomer ran an article about the cleanup effort on the second page of every issue of the *Birmingham News* for an entire week in November 1967.

The publicity Bloomer provided through the *News* was highly effective in drawing attention to the rural cleanup endeavor, and that first meeting began a partnership between McInnis and Bloomer that led to the development of something new for Alabama—a coordinated environmental education program.

Certainly, Bloomer's help with the publicity was priceless, but that publicity was also backed up with action from the AFB's women working in counties across the state. "The county people were marvelous and they knew how to get things done," said McInnis. Collaborating with the AFB's Public Affairs Division, the Women's Committee began holding workshops and seminars across the state to teach county AFB members how to organize local cleanup campaigns. They also provided sample news releases, proclamations, public service announcements, and a pledge that local officials and other stakeholders could sign in support of Rural Cleanup Week.

In addition to promoting Rural Cleanup Week, the women also began surveying their counties to identify illegal dumps, after which they started putting pressure on their county officials to get these eyesores cleaned up.

Through such activities the AFB women and others in local communities were making "sweeping changes" in Alabama's environmental sector, an effort that was fast becoming more than just a project. It was turning into a movement that was garnering attention across the state.

As a January 21, 1968, letter to McInnis from Ed Dannelly, then–

Figure 4. The AEQA's education program sought to teach citizens to take care of their state, from cleaning up trash that littered roadsides, cemeteries, and historical sites—such as this marker at Fort Toulouse—to becoming cleanup activists in their communities. (Courtesy of AEQA.)

editor of the *Andalusia Star-News*, stated: "Having witnessed numerous other efforts, targeting on rural cleanups, over a period of years, it is the judgment of this newspaper that never before has there been the concerted action to bring improvements like you have generated."

Another event that spurred the effort further was the first rural cleanup banquet and statewide recognition program (an event that became a powerful public relations tool in the years to come), which was held in Montgomery on February 5, 1968, as part of the Farm Bureau's "Focus on Action in Farm Bureau" Women's Leadership Conference. Bloomer spoke at this event, declaring, "Nature has given us one of the most beautiful states in the nation, but we have despoiled it." While acknowledging that local officials, teachers, students, principals, health departments, and other groups had certainly been a great part of the effort, Bloomer added with a grin: "Of course, [these folks] also probably had a vision of one hundred thousand farm women coming at them with mops and brooms."

He not only praised the Women's Committee for its efforts in 1967, he ran a follow-up editorial in the *Birmingham News* on February 8, 1968, saying:

> Give some groups the task of eliminating trash piles and other eyesores in rural Alabama, and you might get a lot of hemming and hawing and long-range planning before you get any real results.
>
> Give the same assignment to the women of the Alabama Farm Bureau, and what you get is action—now.

There was no doubt that the movement was spreading across the state, and the women behind it were not shy about taking it further and demanding action from their local officials. For example, members of the Talladega County Women's Committee and County Extension Homemakers Council arranged a meeting with their county commissioners in early March 1968 to lobby for a fee-based pickup service and the creation of two sanitary landfills to accept refuse. During that meeting, Mrs. Ernest Wallace, vice president of the Talladega Homemakers Council, pointed out, "We have over eight hundred members." Perhaps her reminder of the voting power of their group of women hit home. A month later, the Talladega County Commission voted to establish four landfills, one in each county district.

The cleanup effort was also drawing the attention of the US Public Health Service (PHS), a division of the US Department of Health, Education, and Welfare (HEW, now the US Department of Health and Human Services). PHS officials saw Alabama's cleanup campaign as a way to further their efforts to rid the state of the yellow fever–vector mosquito, *Aedes aegypti*, which bred in the water-retaining trash and old tires of illegal dumping areas.

Seizing the opportunity to build on the cleanup campaign's momentum and foster further collaboration among groups, "Principles of Refuse Handling Practice" workshops were held across the state from April 29 through May 3, 1968. Those meetings featured experts from the PHS who spoke on virtually every aspect of solid waste disposal and provided information on how to build and operate sanitary landfill facilities.

Later that month, HEW Project Officer Alfred Chipley announced that the AFB's Women's Committee would receive HEW's first-ever Certificate of Appreciation because, he said in a letter to McInnis, "Your influence, and that of your active county committees, has been strongly felt throughout your state, and your decision to continue rural cleanup as a perpetual project will be of immeasurable value in bringing Alabama to its rightful place as (the) leading state in health and beauty."

As the movement grew, more and more people in all sectors of Alabama society began lining up in support of the cleanup effort, touting it as a way to not only make Alabama healthier and more beautiful but also to increase tourism and other economic development opportunities.

Though the Rural Cleanup Week's first official statewide political supporter, Lurleen Wallace, had passed away in early May 1968, support for the endeavor continued when Albert Brewer, who was lieutenant governor at the time of Wallace's death, assumed the gubernatorial duties. In pledging his support of statewide cleanup efforts, Brewer kept the movement's momentum alive, as did the many grassroots supporters in the state who continued working diligently to clean up their communities.

Figure 5. In the late 1960s, as the rural cleanup effort that later became the AEQA sprang into action, a grassroots coalition of volunteers was already out working diligently in local communities. (Courtesy of the AEQA.)

As the cleanup movement grew, so did the realization that the grassroots effort needed a more viable structure if it were to be sustained. To that end, Bloomer asked the Alabama Legislature's Agriculture Joint Interim Committees to set up a subcommittee to study rural cleanup issues, including air and water pollution. On September 18, 1968, a meeting was held at the Farm Bureau Building

Figure 6. Governor Lurleen Wallace, Alabama's first female governor, was also the first supporter of the woman-led Alabama rural cleanup campaign. (Used with permission from the Alabama Department of Archives and History.)

in Montgomery to officially launch a broader statewide Rural Cleanup Campaign.

During the meeting, it was announced that an Alabama Rural Cleanup Advisory Committee had been formed, with Brewer as its ex-officio chairman, Bloomer as chairman, and McInnis serving as coordinator of the Rural Cleanup Program. The advisory committee also included representatives of nearly every sector of government, education, health, and public service. "The presence of representatives of such a broad spectrum of our population provides ample proof of the growing interest in this worthwhile endeavor," said Brewer during the event, adding, "We have only scratched the surface in seeking a permanent solution to the problem of waste disposal."

As McInnis mustered the Farm Bureau women to the effort, encouraging them to mobilize local groups for action by conducting countywide rural cleanup meetings and creating their own county advisory committees for the Rural Cleanup Program, others were joining the crusade and calling for an expansion of the cleanup program.

In the December 1968 edition of *Alabama Forest Products*, an article quoted Dr. Ira L. Myers, the Alabama state health officer who spoke at the kickoff meeting, as saying: "A changing environment—increasing population growth, rapid movement to cities, growth in industrial areas, and many other conditions—has multiplied the need for a coordinated movement to eliminate the refuse eyesore that is so rapidly spreading, [and] in turn lowering property values and creating health and safety hazards."

Looking back on those days, Brewer noted that Alabama's rural cleanup effort began at an interesting period in both state and national politics. "It was a time of great change and upheaval," he recalled. "People in the 1960s were preoccupied with the Vietnam War, civil and voting rights, and the end of segregation, but at the same time there was a grassroots movement of concern for the environment."

Among those pushing for environmental legislation and controls were members of the Sierra Club and other national groups who were using litigation, political pressure, and demonstrations to draw attention to existing problems. Those pressures led to national legislation to control water and air pollution, meaning that the formation of an environmental quality movement in Alabama fit hand-in-hand with these national advancements.

"We were under a lot of pressure from the federal government to pass legislation to adopt a statute regulating air pollution con-

Figure 7. Following Lurleen Wallace's untimely death, her successor Governor Albert Brewer continued to support the rural cleanup effort. He is pictured here giving the keynote address at one of the Rural Cleanup annual awards luncheons, as John Bloomer, editor of the *Birmingham News* (who helped establish the AEQA), looks on. (Courtesy of the AEQA.)

trol," Brewer recalled. If Alabama did not pass its own bill, the federal government would do it for the state, a threat that brought together a coalition made up of diverse interest groups to develop Alabama's first true environmental laws.

"The bill that passed our legislature was a consensus bill that had involvement from industry and various environmental groups, property owners, and other grassroots groups," Brewer said. And it was sorely needed, he added, noting as one example the air pollution that enveloped and suffocated Birmingham at the time. "I can remember flying into Birmingham on a perfectly sunny day, and the pilots would be flying on instruments because the smog was so thick," he recalled.

Furthermore, according to Brewer, "This (legislation to protect Alabama's environment) was a citizen success story, because if there hadn't been support for it, the control legislation would not have passed. And the support came from so many people," he continued, noting in particular Bloomer, McInnis, and the Farm Bureau. "I don't know what we would have done without that energy and initiative in this area," he said, adding that Alabama women were the primary movers and shakers behind the issue. "Frankly, it was not just a do-good project for these women," he concluded. "It was important to the health and well-being of Alabama people."

In light of all this legislation and change, when the rural cleanup idea came to Brewer's desk, he had no trouble supporting it.

"Martha was my contact with this group," he recalled, noting that he already knew McInnis through her work with Brewer's wife on a first ladies' cookbook. "There was so little that I could do other than offer official support by proclamation and publicity, but if Martha was interested in something like this I would do anything I could to help her. I believed in what she was doing and was confident that she would not go off half-cocked on it."

3
"Sweeping" Change

Women's Rural Cleanup Campaign Expands

"There's a large broom with many pushers sweeping over the state. And here's a warning to beware, lest you be swept up in the biggest cleanup effort Alabama has seen in a long time." These words, written by the AFB's Department of Information Director Charles McCay in an article in the January 1969 issue of *AREA* magazine, captured the popular metaphor of brooms (and mops) becoming the tools for "sweeping" changes in Alabama that were being led by a group of ardent and energized Farm Bureau women.

"Broom is Proving Formidable Weapon" was the headline for a March 12, 1969, article in the *Birmingham News* by Thomas F. Hill, who went on to say:

> The broom, like the pen, may also be mightier than the sword.
>
> The cloud of dust swept up by the brooms has spread to the innermost sections of urban Alabama and the legislative halls in Montgomery.

Figure 8. Brooms and mops became symbols for the
"sweeping" changes under way through Alabama's Rural
Cleanup campaign, which was led by the Alabama Farm
Bureau Federation's women. By the time this image
appeared on the cover of an Alabama Rural Electric
Association publication, the cleanup effort had been
effectively launched and was gaining both attention and
traction throughout the state. (Courtesy of the AEQA.)

There was no doubt: the rural cleanup effort had expanded from
a campaign to beautify rural Alabama into a program that was addressing a wide array of issues, ranging from beautification and its
potential to increase tourism in the state to improving the health
and lives of both urban and rural residents by controlling air and

water pollution and providing solutions to a major problem of the era, the disposal of solid waste.

By early 1969, part of that "sweeping" effort was being guided not just by the AFB women but also by a newly formed state Rural Cleanup Advisory Committee, which held its first official meeting February 6, 1969, in Montgomery to discuss methods for grassroots action, techniques for informing and involving people, and means of rallying community action behind the plan.

On March 5, 1969, the first in a series of eight regional advi sory committee meetings was held in Birmingham, during which the AFB's President J. D. Hays furthered the cause by saying that the Rural Cleanup Program "has become the motivating force for county and city governing bodies, law enforcement officials, educators, legislators, and others to discuss solid waste disposal in Alabama." The area meetings also built greater awareness of the need for landfills and other solid waste disposal options in the state, as seen shortly in letters that started coming in from across Alabama asking for help in cleaning up local communities.

Several local governments began instituting solid waste disposal programs of their own. Calhoun County, for example, started a containerized garbage program with drop-off locations throughout the district, and Talladega County established a countywide sanitary landfill system while destroying illegal roadside dumpsites. But to make a real difference, the Alabama Legislature had to take action.

To that end, Talladega State Representative Phil Smith called for legislation that would "untie the hands of county officials." A March 6, 1969, *Birmingham News* article also called for state legislation to "provide legal authority for county and local cleanup programs."

Hilmer Jones, chairman of the Environmental Health Division of the Alabama Cooperative Extension Service, underscored the need for legislation, saying it was needed to "clarify the powers of the municipalities and counties to set up collection and disposal procedures." The hue and cry resulted in action when Alabama Senator Walter C. Givhan, a powerful legislator from Dallas County, sponsored a bill establishing just such a law. The Farm Bureau's women were instrumental in drafting the bill—the Solid Waste Disposal Law of 1969—which passed in the Alabama Legislature's 1969 regular session and became Alabama's (and one of the nation's) first solid waste disposal bill.

Though the new law required county commissions to spend money in enacting the law, the response was generally positive, and because this was a landmark bill for the state and the nation, folks in Washington took notice and came to Alabama to find out how such a political feat had been accomplished.

The success of the program also brought Alabama positive attention from other national groups, including the US Chamber of Commerce. In 1969, its director of public affairs, Dorothy L. Fletchner, visited Alabama and met with the AFB women who were behind much of this change. Soon thereafter she ran an article in the spring 1969 edition of her national newsletter, *Spotlight on Women in Public Affairs*, proclaiming Alabama's cleanup effort as "one of the finest volunteer programs at work in America" and citing the outstanding work of its women leaders.

The year's accomplishments were honored on October 1, 1969, during the second annual Alabama cleanup banquet held in Montgomery. The event drew some six hundred attendees and featured not only an awards program but also nationally prominent speakers, such as US Interior Secretary Walter J. Hickel, American Farm Bureau Federation President Charles B. Shuman, and US Congressmen Bill Dickinson and John Buchanan, Sr.

During the banquet, Hickel praised Alabama's efforts, stating that "I think that you are leading the nation, showing the rest of America the way" and adding that Alabama's cleanup and beautification program "appears to be the most exciting and successful effort of its kind."

"You know that we cannot wait for government," he continued. "Private citizens must take the initiative—be aggressive and lead the way. That is exactly what your Farm Bureau Women's Committee did."

In May 1969, Alabama's Rural Cleanup Committee also began a long and productive relationship with Keep America Beautiful, Inc., (KAB) when McInnis was asked to make a presentation at a KAB workshop in Columbia, South Carolina. Later that year Alabama won the first of what would become many KAB awards for the state and for local county and city projects. KAB also began sending national staff members to Alabama to learn more about how the state was making such remarkable strides in its cleanup efforts and perhaps apply those ideas to other states and communities across the country.

Tuscaloosa was one of only two counties across the nation to receive the award that year, and Dot Smith, who had been a leader both at the state level and within her local cleanup effort (she served as the chairwoman of the county Women's Committee and also worked on the Tuscaloosa County Beautification Council, which she later chaired), went to New York to accept the award and make a presentation about the council's work to conference attendees.

According to McInnis, Smith was one of a number of Farm Bureau women who, thanks in large part to their work with the Rural Cleanup Program, blossomed personally and professionally. "When I first met Dot she didn't even drive," recalled McInnis. Within a short time, though, Smith not only obtained her driver's license but became a rural mail carrier, a job that, like Tompkins's, helped further impress upon Smith the need for rural cleanup.

"I had a long route and was able to see the trash dumps, and I

Figure 9. Many of the women who led the charge to clean up Alabama went on to win national accolades, including myriad awards from Keep America Beautiful, Inc. Pictured (from left) at the 1971 KAB awards event are Martha McInnis, Mrs. J. W. Bragg Jr. of Madison County, and Dot Smith of Tuscaloosa County. (Courtesy of the AEQA.)

guess that's what made me really want to take the thing on," said Smith, who described herself as "Chairman of Cleanup" and went on to be elected to the Tuscaloosa County Board of Education, serving on it for eighteen years from 1986 to 2004 and ultimately becoming the board's chairman.

Another shining star of the Women's Committee was Gay Lang-

Figure 10. In December 1973, AEQA Executive Vice President Martha McInnis was awarded the Mrs. Lyndon B. Johnson Award, the Keep America Beautiful campaign's top volunteer award created in honor of the former first lady. It was one of many KAB awards that the AEQA and its corps of volunteers won through the years. Alabama finally won so many awards it was retired from competition and inducted into KAB's President's Circle. (Courtesy of the AEQA.)

ley, who eventually became the first woman elected to the Alabama Farm Bureau State Board of Directors and was also elected to the Talladega Board of Education. Other women, such as Murrah Young of Randolph County, were also literally able to expand their horizons. Young had never traveled outside the state of Alabama before she was invited to represent her county at the national KAB awards ceremony in New York City in 1967.

"This was a time when women were not listened to," said McInnis, who had experienced that herself as a career woman in a male-dominated world. "So many of them were timid and shy, but they were not timid or shy when it came to this project."

"I think working on the Rural Cleanup Program gave these women a cause they could believe in and a platform through which they could develop their skills as public speakers and as leaders in their communities," she continued. "I saw it over and over again. The program gave them a calling card and pride within their communities. And, working together, they networked and stimulated one another, and the recognition they received was rewarding for them." McInnis concluded, "We talk about empowering women today, but I can attest to the fact that this idea is not a new thing."

4
Building an Environmental Conscience and Structure

As the decade of the 1970s began, more and more Alabama communities joined the effort to clean up the state, and McInnis and her band of volunteers continued to expand their efforts and cause within the state and beyond. Their sense of purpose was also filtering into state government, as signaled by an increase in environmental legislation being brought to state lawmakers, much of which was championed by State Representative Phil Smith.

He and other legislators began introducing bills to address myriad environmental issues, from strengthening the state's anti-litter law to protecting Alabama's scenic beauty through the establishment of mini-wilderness areas, the protection of caverns, caves and scenic rivers, and the development of scenic trails. Other bills were also proposed, relating to using and controling pesticides, setting new standards for solid waste disposal, allowing bonds to be issued to finance pollution control equipment, and regulating strip mining.

The legislature's efforts and the role of the Alabama Rural Cleanup Advisory Committee in helping develop much of the new legislation also drew more national attention. In 1971, US Secretary of the Interior Rogers C. B. Morton came to Alabama for the annual Rural Cleanup Banquet and stated that the Alabama Rural Cleanup Advisory Committee was responsible "for some of the best state environmental legislation in America."

While much was being accomplished, there was still so much more that could be done to clean up Alabama and protect its environment. Inevitably, discussions began in earnest about how to turn this growing grassroots crusade into a more organized movement.

In 1971, Representative Smith called for the establishment of an "environmental council" to act as a clearinghouse for all pollution control measures, saying, "It would include everything from water and air pollution problems to anti-litter and strip mining control measures." For her part, McInnis was also making a case for a "sensible, long-range plan in connection with the environmental quality control programs," adding, "Alabama's come a long way, but there is still a long way to go."

In an effort to take the movement to new levels and, realizing that doing so would require a more organized, sustainable approach, McInnis and others began looking for ways to establish a permanent, long-range environmental quality program.

In 1971 while on a Farm Bureau trip to Washington, DC, McInnis had put a bug in the ear of US Representative Bill Dickinson, saying, "If there is ever any environmental legislation funding that becomes available we would appreciate it if you let us know." Hope for such monies was dim, admitted McInnis: "That was before the days when environmentalism took off." But about a year later, a big package arrived for her from Dickinson's office, so big that she let it linger on her desk for weeks before even opening it.

When she took it home one weekend and began going through it, though, she realized it contained an announcement about grants available through the National Environmental Education Act of 1970, grants that provided funding for the development of a state master environmental education plan. The deadline for submitting a proposal was only a week away and much work needed to be done to qualify for the grant, including writing the proposal and creating a nonprofit organization to administer the award if and when it was received.

"Mr. Hays (the AFB's president) was in Kansas City, and I got him on the phone that Monday and asked about submitting a proposal," said McInnis. He told her to enlist the help of the AFB's lawyer, Ted Jackson, with the Rushton, Stakely, Johnston, and Garrett law firm, to get the organization incorporated as a 501(c)3 nonprofit named the Alabama Environmental Quality Association (AEQA).

To help guide the AEQA, the state also formally established the Alabama Environmental Quality Advisory Council (AEQC). Its members included John Bloomer, Hays, State Health Officer Dr. Ira Myers, Alabama Superintendent of Education Earnest Stone, and others who could help connect the AEQA with other organizations, from civic and Scout groups to the Alabama Broadcasters Association. "The strength of that council was its ability to accomplish things, and its members did not come with their own agendas," said McInnis. "They were generous with their time and tried to figure out ways to make it work."

With this framework in place, McInnis began working frantically to write the proposal, a process that was new to her. "I called a few states that had done similar work (Colorado and Massachusetts in particular), then sat down and wrote a proposal," she said. "It was a long process to get it typed and in the proper form," she recalled, but with the help of AFB typists working overtime, the application was completed and postmarked by midnight on the deadline.

Though the proposal was in the pipeline, McInnis soon discovered that her work was not finished. She was told by Thomas Bobo, then-superintendent of the Montgomery Public School System,

"'You know it's not going to get anywhere if you don't bird dog it,'" recalled McInnis. "I didn't know what 'bird dogging it' meant."

Thankfully, Bloomer and US Congressman John Buchanan from Birmingham did know what "bird dogging it" entailed, and they, with help from Dickinson, arranged for McInnis and Bloomer to come to DC and meet with Robert Gilkey—director of the Office of Education's Environmental Education Program—to advocate for the proposal. "We were so eager," McInnis remembered. "When we got to DC, we had a meeting that afternoon with Buchanan and Dickinson and rehearsed our presentation."

The next morning Bloomer, McInnis, and Buchanan (Dickinson couldn't go because he had been called to the White House to meet with Henry Kissinger) set off to see Gilkey. But when they got there, they were told that no appointment for them was on the calendar and that Gilkey had a meeting out of the building.

"Buchanan stepped forward and said 'I gave up a congressional committee meeting to keep this appointment so Gilkey can talk to us now or he can come to my office later,'" recalled McInnis. "Gilkey stormed out of his office with his briefcase but turned around and went back into his office to talk to us," she said. Despite its tumultuous beginning, that meeting "put our foot in the door, and we ultimately got the grant to establish a state environmental education master plan."

5
Structuring for the Future

While waiting to hear about the National Environmental Education grant, McInnis, Bloomer, and others in the state continued to assemble support for environmental quality efforts, finding another strong ally in the governor's office.

George Wallace, who was again governor after defeating Albert Brewer in a close and heated election the previous year, proclaimed April 1972 as "Environmental Quality Month," the first of what was to be many years when an entire month, not just a week or weekend, was set aside to focus on environmental quality issues and projects.

"Our citizens are becoming increasingly aware of the delicate balance between the full use and appreciation of Alabama's natural resources and scenic wealth and the loss of these material and aesthetic treasures through the lack of adequate protective measures," Wallace said when he announced the proclamation.

McInnis and Bloomer were also working to fully establish a structure for the AEQA and AEQC, a plan that included the formation of regional Alabama Environmental Quality Councils that Bloomer and McInnis felt were key to furthering grassroots engagement in

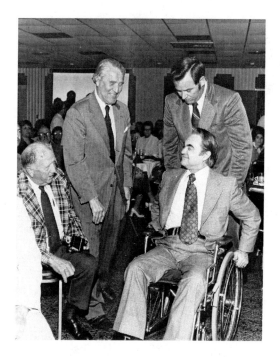

Figure 11. George Wallace, pictured here with Wernher
von Braun at the 1975 annual awards luncheon, was
a staunch supporter of the AEQA. (Courtesy of the
AEQA.)

the cause. As Bloomer noted at the time, "If our state committee
is duplicated on a regional basis the impact will be amazingly em-
phasized."

Members of these councils were carefully chosen to represent a
wide range of interests in each district. They were often movers and
shakers in their communities and vocations and included city council and school board members, university professors, civic leaders,
and many others who had connections with myriad groups that
could be helpful in the AEQA's work.

Figure 12. As projects of the Alabama Environmental Quality Association began to take off across the state, AEQA Field Representative Frank Filgo and other staff members visited communities in every Alabama county to find out more about their environmental challenges and further organize the swelling grassroots movement. (Courtesy of the AEQA.)

The council districts were set up to mirror Alabama Development Office Planning Districts, which allowed the regional councils to establish closer links with the Regional Planning Commission and governmental agencies. "Since many programs that fund community environmental projects require regional approval," said McInnis, "the Alabama Development Districts, as legal entities, could provide that assistance."

In addition to the eight regional councils, the plan also established eleven interest groups in the areas of education, youth, communication and media, conservation, community improvement, civic and service clubs, city/county/state government, business and industry, health, rural, and legislative.

In May 1972, a statewide meeting was held to announce the formation of these councils. Among its attendees was Dixon Hubbard, a USDA Extension Service representative who was in the state to tout the USDA's newly established Environmental Trust Program, a system Hubbard said was intended to "challenge every source of pollution, ugliness and blight" in America. He praised Alabama's ongoing environmental endeavors, saying, "I don't know of any other state in the nation that is already better organized along those lines than Alabama. We want to tie the USDA Trust Program to this already established organization."

Shortly after this meeting, on June 22, 1972, it was announced that the AEQA had indeed been awarded a forty-three thousand-dollar National Environmental Education Act grant to establish a statewide evaluation and dissemination program for environmental problems and pollution controls and "pinpoint and help solve problems in virtually every sector of Alabama."

In an August 4, 1972, story in the *Birmingham News*, Bloomer announced that the grant would be used to develop an Environmental Education Master Plan for Alabama to "better all aspects of Alabama's environment."

The next month, in an article in the September edition of *Alabama Farm Bureau News*, McInnis lauded the progress made during the previous five years stating that the Rural Cleanup Program and the awarding of this grant "exemplifies two rules of mankind. First, worthwhile programs are like the small acorn planted in the Fall that over the years matures into the full grown sturdy oak. Secondly, worthwhile movements that benefit all mankind are never the results of one individual but rather the diligent work of numerous persons dedicated to a cause that is greater than themselves. No other movement has given such opportunity for bringing so many individuals' good impulses to the front and inspiring them to reach higher levels of achievement in effecting environmental quality. We have the opportunity to improve our past record and enlarge our cooperation with others for a common cause."

On November 8, 1972, a luncheon was held at the Jefferson Davis Hotel in Montgomery to officially launch the master plan project and to lay out the program's administrative structure. Under that configuration, the AEQC served as the advisory arm while the AEQA was the boots-on-the-ground part of the organization, executing its day-to-day operations.

The primary objectives for the AEQC and AEQA were: "Work for a solution of problems concerning man's relationship with his natural and man-made surroundings; encourage the preservation of Alabama's natural beauty and environment through a program of public education; develop among Alabama residents pride in their communities and state; encourage and assist in the development of voluntary community development; promote the establishment of local volunteer environmental programs; allow the full use of the environment of each present generation without adverse effects on full use by each future generation."

Bloomer was named chairman of the AEQC, with Governor George Wallace as ex-officio chairman. The council's membership included some sixty people representing a "divergent array of interests and backgrounds," such as garden club officers, public health personnel, educators, industrialists, university officials, and environmental specialists. "Pooling their own unique resources, council members come to the same table and focus on the environmental problems common to all people of the state. In this manner, the quality of life in Alabama is placed in the hands of lay citizens," the plan stated.

It also spelled out the AEQC's mission to serve as "the coordinating agency through which citizens, public and private organizations, state and local governments, and business and industry work together to prevent pollution, to insure clean, attractive neighborhoods, highways, parks, lakes, streams, and historic sites, and to foster quality living in general."

The AEQA staff was also announced. It consisted of Bruce Gilliland, who would serve as the master plan's project director; McInnis, who was named executive director of the project while keeping her duties at the Farm Bureau; and Carolyn Dunlavy, who would serve as project secretary. This three-person staff would be involved in "a myriad of service endeavors." Top among these was spending the coming year surveying the environmental views of the people of Alabama, followed by structuring a plan tailored to their needs and lifestyles. The staff would also set up a clearinghouse of information, help plan the annual awards event, and work with Keep America Beautiful and other organizations.

They would also establish a speakers' bureau; facilitate the development of recycling centers and environmental education programs in local communities; build relationships with institutions of higher-education; operate a resource service; exchange information with national professional education groups with goals similar to those of the AEQA; and revise the environmental master plan through public meetings every five years.

Although numerous other states had developed plans for environmental education, Alabama's plan was unique because, rather than work through formal education outlets such as schools, it was set up as a community-wide environmental education approach that engaged citizens from all walks of life. The underlying philosophy of Alabama's plan was for it to be a truly grassroots program through which Alabamians could make decisions about their environment using factual information.

Thus, the plan sought to accomplish one basic goal: "the development of an environmentally literate citizenry, one which can effect change in environmental attitudes, values, and patterns of behavior. It is designed to prevent, identify, and solve community environmental problems, resulting in a higher quality of life and a sound development of this region of America."

With a structure and the grant funding in place, the effort to develop a master plan for environmental education for Alabama was under way—the first step toward allowing Alabama's environmental quality movement to truly put down roots.

6
Formulating a Master Plan

The first regional meeting to begin developing the master plan was held in Montgomery on January 9, 1973, followed by others throughout the month in each of the state's other regions. These town meeting–style events allowed anyone and everyone to speak their minds and offer input, continuing the grassroots-driven mission begun almost a decade before by Lance Tompkins.

McInnis and Gilliland also began traveling across the state presenting programs to community and civic groups. They carried with them a commitment to help citizens effect change in their own communities by banding together for the "greater good."

In an effort to gauge environmental attitudes in Alabama, the AEQA conducted an extensive survey that was mailed to some two thousand six hundred Alabama residents and also ran in newspapers statewide. The results of the survey, which were released in late 1973, offered insights into the environmental mood and awareness of the state's citizens. Among the findings were:

Air pollution is Alabama's most pressing environmental
problem, followed by water pollution, littering, and solid
waste.

The most effective solution to the state's environmental
troubles is strict enforcement of existing legislation.

Alabama citizens are willing to make sacrifices to achieve a
higher standard of living through improvements in the
environment.

Seventy-five percent of the respondents also said that they were
willing to pay higher prices for products so manufacturers could in-
stall pollution control devices, drive smaller cars, and use less elec-
tricity. In other words, Alabamians not only cared about environmental issues, they were willing to tackle the problems associated
with pollution, energy conservation, and myriad other challenges,
and they were willing to make sacrifices to do so.

Meanwhile, the regional councils were also busy effecting change
in their local communities, something they viewed as an ongoing
and vital undertaking. Those sentiments were illustrated by Dot
Smith, who had by then become the cochairman of her regional
council, when she said, "This is what I have found: That you can't
ever let up. It's our job to help fit the pieces of the puzzle together."

When George Wallace again proclaimed April 1973 as Alabama
Environmental Quality Month, he noted: "The people of Alabama
have long demonstrated a deep respect for the handiwork of God
and a genuine concern for enhancing the quality of life for our citizens." He went on to say that, through the "participatory democracy" manifested in the AEQA and its local and regional leaders,
"Alabama is fast becoming a national leader in the grassroots movement to preserve and protect our rich bounty of natural resources,
and attack the root causes of pollution."

After miles of travel and hours of time spent talking to and taking the pulse of Alabama citizens' views on environmental issues, the Alabama Environmental Education Master Plan was completed and officially released in November 1973 during a luncheon at the Farm Bureau building. Still, although completion of the plan was a significant step toward a more organized environmental education program for the state, McInnis and Bloomer knew that the blueprint would be of no value unless it was implemented. Thus, the hunt began to find a source of continued funding for the AEQA to administer the master plan.

One option, suggested by Red Bamberg, who was then director of the Alabama Development Office (ADO), was to secure state funding for the organization. A likely source of that funding was the state's federal revenue sharing dollars, federal tax revenue that was at the time returned to the states to use at their discretion and, in Alabama, was distributed through the ADO.

To get those monies, however, McInnis and Bloomer needed to meet with then-Alabama finance director Taylor Hardin before the budget was set in July. In June, Hardin was attending the Southern Governors' Association conference, which was being held in Point Clear, Alabama. McInnis and Bloomer flew down to the Gulf Coast and were escorted to a private home where Hardin, an avid tennis fan, was watching that year's Wimbledon tennis tournament. Between tennis matches, McInnis and Bloomer kept up a constant conversation with Hardin about the AEQA. Before the day was done, Hardin committed one hundred seventy-five thousand dollars in revenue sharing money to the AEQA, an allotment justified by the fact that there were no state agencies at the time set up to tackle many of the state's environmental issues and needs. "We were filling a void in the areas of health and conservation—things such as promoting recycling and establishing public trails—because the state did not have a staff position or an agency assigned to do this work," said McInnis. Though that changed in later years when the Department of Conservation and Natural Resources and other state agencies began to commit personnel to such jobs, during its tenure the AEQA filled many of these gaps.

Still, the allocation raised more than a few eyebrows and hackles among some groups—particularly other environmental groups and activists in the state who felt the monies would be better spent on other organizations and who were suspicious of the AEQA's close ties to Wallace and the Farm Bureau. According to McInnis, the AEQA was indeed well connected, which proved to be an advantage at the time. The AFB, for example, not only provided McInnis and her staff with office space but also allowed her to spend time working on the project while still an AFB employee, an arrangement that helped satisfy the AEQA's in-kind matching monies for the grant.

"It also opened doors in a lot of respects because the Farm Bureau had the structure in place to navigate the state's political system," she said. "But I can truly say that we never felt pressure from Governor Wallace, the Farm Bureau, or any other organization. Ever. And none of them ever stopped us from tackling big issues, which is frankly amazing."

7
A Dream Team

The AEQA's First Staff

With the release of the master plan and with funding in place from revenue sharing monies, the AEQA was finally able to hire a full-time staff. Among those staff positions was an executive director, a project/field service director to work with the regional councils, a communications manager, and an office manager.

McInnis, who had been splitting her time between her AFB and AEQA roles, was faced with a big decision: stay with the Farm Bureau, where by that time she had worked for seven years, or move over full time to the AEQA as its executive director. "I will never forget talking to Mr. Hays about that," McInnis said, adding that Hays told her, "There are a lot of men that would give their right arm to take that program. You might want to think about it."

Hays, said McInnis, recognized that she could do much more than she was being given the opportunity to do at the Farm Bureau. "He was good at reading people's abilities and he was a people-builder," she said, adding that his confidence in her was a great compliment. And so, with Hays's encouragement, McInnis became executive director of the AEQA in 1972, a move she said "changed my whole career."

Carolyn Dunlavy, who had already been working on staff as the master plan was being developed, stayed on as office manager. Nancy Callahan from Tuscaloosa was hired as the AEQA's communications specialist in December 1973 and Frank Filgo joined the staff in January 1974 as the project director, coming from a position with the Boy Scouts of America in Montgomery.

According to McInnis, this collection of talented people on the staff was remarkable: "Finding the right people made all the difference." In her view, "That team was undoubtedly the most dedicated and had an instinctive ability to carry out the master plan. It was quite phenomenal what we were able to do."

More specifically, "Carolyn was a master organizer," said McInnis. "She had a lot of intuition, a broad knowledge base, and she was always willing to go the extra mile to get things done. And she encouraged others to do that too. She was so good at stimulating other members of the staff."

Callahan, who McInnis said possessed exceptional writing skills and a keen sense of what was "news," recalled that she came to the job somewhat by accident. "I applied for a job at the *Birmingham News*," she said, "but at the time there were no openings." However, the senior editor at the *News* who interviewed Callahan suggested another job—one as communications manager for an environmental organization that the paper's managing editor, John Bloomer, was helping launch.

"It caught me off guard when the editor suggested I get involved with an environmental group," said Callahan, though in retrospect it was a great fit for a young woman who viewed the natural world as "a form of passion and spirituality." Indeed, "I had been a natu-

Figure 13. As part of the AEQA's master plan, regional environmental councils were developed across the state, with representatives from those communities uniting to lead their local cleanup and environmental education efforts. Then-Governor George Wallace (seated), who was a strong supporter of the AEQA, is pictured here looking at the regional council map with (from left) Verda Horne of Mobile County and AEQA Executive Vice President Martha McInnis. (Courtesy of the AEQA.)

ralist all my life," she said. "I grew up on the remains of my grand-parents' old farm and inherited a love for land from both sides of my family." A grassroots movement appealed to her as well: "It was a way that citizens could act out a democracy, other than voting and paying taxes. It was a form of democracy in action."

For his part, Filgo heard about the project director job through a coworker at the Boy Scouts of America and applied, even though he came to the position with no environmental background. "Frank has such a good sense of humor, and he was a good reader of people who could convince people to join the cause, which made what he did for us unique," said McInnis. "If he said he would do something, you could count on it, and he would do anything you'd ask him to, too, like the time we accidentally threw away some documents and he got in a dumpster to retrieve them."

According to Filgo, working with the AEQA deepened his own appreciation for environmental issues. "I think I had to learn to spell 'environment,' but I quickly gained a greater appreciation for the environment and gained an understanding of the tradeoffs we are forced to make," he said.

Despite their diverse backgrounds, McInnis, Dunlavy, Callahan, and Filgo quickly crystalized as a team, in part because of McInnis's passion for their work ("Martha was a fireball and her enthusiasm was contagious," said Dunlavy) but also because they each brought their own talents and passion to their jobs.

"We had a great staff of people, hard workers, dedicated, committed to what we were doing," said Callahan. "That commitment made the program worthwhile for the individual staff members. We could always count on one another."

"We were a close-knit group," said Filgo. "Each staff member had his or her specific responsibilities, and we respected the talents and skills that each contributed."

"The implementation of all the programs was a challenge and at times the responsibility was overwhelming," said Dunlavy. "Everything was a learning process, but it is amazing what we did with such a small staff. We learned that perseverance was tantamount," she said, noting that she and the rest of the staff truly believed in what they were doing. "You've got to believe to make something successful."

And as Dunlavy noted, the core team was backed up with scores of volunteers. "It was absolutely a grassroots organization," she said, "that would not have happened without the volunteers across the state. Those people helped us meet the objectives."

"We were trying to bring about a common sense approach to the discussion of the environment," said Filgo. "We were trying to build consensus, and input from the citizenry was our driving force. We were building an organization from the ground up and we all wanted what was best for Alabama."

"Recruiting volunteers and planning activities were key parts of my responsibilities, and I really enjoyed working with community leaders," he added. "I think I drove every mile of every road in Alabama during my five years with the AEQA. But even in some of the most remote parts of Alabama, community leaders were hard at work trying to make a better life for all. These were the leaders we were seeking."

"I had the opportunity to meet people from all walks of life," he continued. "When building an organization, you first start with good people. Alabama is blessed with good people."

Callahan agreed, saying that while so many people in communities helped with AEQA programs, the Farm Bureau members, particularly the women, built such a strong foundation for the AEQA perhaps because they, too, believed in what they were doing. "Maybe those farmers were naturalists and had never thought about it," she said. "But it makes sense to me that certain aspects of environmentalism would come from farmers and their spouses and children, people who have a connection to the land."

Dunlavy also credited George Wallace and the connections he provided to Montgomery's political powerbrokers for much of their success. "His regular involvement meant a lot," she said.

While Wallace may not have considered himself an environmentalist, Callahan felt that he strongly believed in the basic principle of the AEQA. "I think he was an advocate of grassroots programs putting causes into action," she said. "He was a believer in the potential of the groundswell of the grassroots and what could happen within a grassroots movement." And, while the AEQA's connection with Wallace and AFB drew fire, Callahan noted that "a lot of what we did transcended political issues and disagreements."

"It was a good balance, and the AEQA was instrumental in laying a strong groundwork and bringing environmental issues to the forefront," said Dunlavy, who added that all the staff members were passionate about their work and their commitment to the environment. So with a small but dedicated staff in place, the AEQA set to work.

8

Big Issues, Big Names, Big Ideas

With a full-time staff in place, the AEQA began addressing a broad array of resource management and environmental issues, ranging from recycling to clear-cutting, pesticide use to strip mining, and many others, all based on the unique needs of each Alabama community.

According to Frank Filgo, those needs varied greatly across the state; accordingly, the AEQA tried to address each one in turn. "Surface mining was a big issue in Northwest Alabama," he recalled. "Water pollution was a concern in the Mobile area. In the rural areas, solid waste disposal was the big problem."

One of the big issues of the time, both in Alabama and across the nation, was the energy crisis. The AEQA tackled it in part by working with the Alabama Energy Management Board to conduct a survey gauging what Alabama citizens thought about energy conservation challenges.

The results of that survey, which were released in May 1974, illustrated the diversity of attitudes held by Alabamians as they faced the energy crisis. A primary concern they voiced was the lack of gasoline, though they were split on how to address the problem—about half did not see rationing and other controls as the answer, while the other half saw such measures as the only viable solution. Knowing this helped governmental agencies come up with policies to address the crisis—from encouraging car pools to lowering the highway speed limits—but also helped the AEQA better target its programming, all the while prioritizing education as the primary mission. The association was poised to do so by developing an extensive clearinghouse of information on many environmental topics, by hosting seminars across the state on a variety of issues, and by going to communities to get feedback and spread knowledge on everything from community beautification to hazardous waste disposal. These seminars were effective and vital to the AEQA's work.

"They were a way to bring grassroots people in and educate them about the environmental issues of the state," said Nancy Callahan, citing as an example a series of environmental law seminars conducted with the help of then-Attorney General Bill Baxley to address environmental law enforcement matters. During the seminars, attendees not only learned about the enforcement issues but also about how to report problems.

The AEQA also offered opportunities for Alabamians to gain a nationwide perspective on environmental concerns by bringing in nationally prominent speakers for its awards luncheons. For example, American Broadcast Corporation Science Editor Jules Bergman, the keynote speaker for the 1974 environmental quality awards luncheon, brought a national perspective on water quality issues.

The 1975 awards luncheon featured yet another nationally acclaimed scientist—Wernher von Braun, the German and later American aerospace engineer and space architect who was considered one of the "Fathers of Rocket Science."

According to McInnis, von Braun's message was futuristic, as he talked about how technology could be used to protect and support the environment. Von Braun cited the potential use of satel-

Figure 14. Werhner von Braun, the noted aerospace
engineer and space architect, was one of many high-
profile keynote speakers featured at the AEQA's
annual awards luncheons. Here, he is pictured
speaking at the 1975 luncheon, where he touted the
use of technology to help preserve the environment, a
now commonplace idea that was quite revolutionary
at the time. (Courtesy of the AEQA.)

lite technology to help in agriculture, land-use issues, and even in
the preservation of old buildings as one of many positive uses for
technology—all uses that are today almost commonplace but at the
time were virtually unknown.

When US Secretary of the Interior Thomas S. Kleppe gave the
keynote address at the 1976 awards luncheon, he cited the energy

crisis as a major national challenge. Though he was an advocate for increasing production of oil, gas, and coal to end the crisis, he also warned that these resources must be used wisely, noting that the challenge facing the nation was "development of generally abundant resources in an environmentally acceptable manner."

The tradition of the annual awards luncheon featuring nationally prominent speakers also tapped into the artistic community. For instance, for the 1977 banquet, the keynote speaker was artist Hubert Shuptrine, who had collaborated with writer and poet James Dickey on the award winning book *Jericho: The South Beheld*.

During his address, Shuptrine eloquently connected art to the environment, stating that his mission as an artist was "to make you aware of the beauty and unique qualities that cannot go unnoticed without losing your equilibrium, flattening your own aesthetic sense."

Though the AEQA was having quite an impact in Alabama, it was evident to McInnis and others in the organization that a regional environmental education effort was also needed. They concluded that providing a forum for such collaboration was the way forward, leading to the establishment of the *EnviroSouth* magazine, a publication that covered environmental issues in Alabama, Florida, Georgia, Louisiana, Mississippi, North Carolina, South Carolina, and Tennessee.

The magazine's mission was to spotlight "the South's quality of life and balanced growth through a practical application of its many resources." And it was designed to be a forum that "should appeal to anyone in the southland who has an appreciation of the environment and a concern to improve it." McInnis saw the venture as a "new and innovative approach to environmental journalism: "There was a need for environmental journalism because there was no way to disseminate the information that people needed to know."

EnviroSouth, one of the nation's early leaders in promoting and developing environmental journalism, soon became an award-winning publication with a devoted readership.

Figure 15. Among the luminaries who came to the AEQA awards luncheon in its later years was artist Hubert Shuptrine, pictured here at an art show and reception hosted at the State Capitol Rotunda with George Wallace. Shuptrine's art and the words of writer and poet James Dickey were featured in the book *Jericho: The South Beheld*. (Courtesy of the AEQA.)

According to McInnis, the magazine had a correspondent in each state and gathered together a stable of talented writers, some of whom were already famous and others who went on to gain fame, including one who became a Nieman Foundation fellow.

Bylines in the magazine included the governors of each southeastern state as well as Kettering Foundation President David Mathews, Alabama folklorist and storyteller Kathryn Tucker Windham, and Ann Cotrell Free, a poet, novelist, and journalist who served as *EnviroSouth*'s Washington correspondent.

According to McInnis, Free was a "true environmentalist" who

Figure 16. In 1977, the AEQA established a regional presence with the launching of *EnviroSouth* magazine, a pioneer of environmental journalism for the region. The magazine's launch eventually led to the creation of EnviroSouth, Inc., a not-for-profit regional environmental organization. (Courtesy of the AEQA.)

also broke barriers for women in journalism. She was the first female Washington correspondent for the *New York Herald Tribune, Newsweek,* and the *Chicago Sun* and later went on to work for other prestigious national newspapers. She initiated the establishment of the Rachel Carson National Wildlife Refuge, received the Rachel Carson Legacy Award in 1988, and was inducted into the Virginia Communications Hall of Fame in 1996.

Many other celebrated Alabama journalists and writers also worked with the magazine, including Wayne Greenhaw, Frank Sikora, Dr. Ed Givhan, and Gillis Morgan, who served as a contributing editor for *EnviroSouth* from 1980 through 1987.

Morgan, who as a reporter working during the days of the Civil Rights Movement had witnessed and reported on a great deal of change and turmoil in Alabama, recalled that "environmentalism was a very emotional issue at the time." But, he added, *EnviroSouth* navigated those issues with finesse, something he credited McInnis for making happen. "Martha was a smart person and was good at getting the right people together and getting them to talk," he said.

From that magazine also came EnviroSouth, Inc., a nonprofit founded in 1979 as "an endeavor which could well become a working blueprint through which democracy in our part of the country can be restored in its purest form."

EnviroSouth magazine went out of print in 1989, but its impact was far-reaching while it was in existence, as the publication served as a major source of environmental information for the entire region.

9
Blazing New Trails at Home and in the Region

Since its beginning, the AEQA was involved in the preservation of scenic and historic trails and sites, from working to help establish the Chinnabee Silent Trail in Talladega National Forest as a National Recreational Trail to helping kick-start an effort to clean up and preserve Old Cahawba, the site of Alabama's first state capitol in Dallas County. But among its greatest and longest-lasting contributions to historic and natural preservation was its work in establishing the Bartram Trail Conference.

Beginning in 1773, American naturalist William Bartram spent four years traveling through the South, recording his encounters in writings and drawings of the region's native flora, fauna, and people. His field notes and drawings were published in a 1791 book that is today known as *Bartram's Travels*.

In the early 1970s, almost two hundred years after the publication of *Bartram's Travels* and as the United States' own bicentennial celebration was approaching, a number of groups in each of the eight states along Bartram's route—North Carolina, South Carolina,

Figure 17. William Bartram's travels in the 1800s brought him through eight southeastern states, including parts of Alabama. This map shows his route through Alabama. (Courtesy of the AEQA.)

Figure 18. A one-mile walking trail in Tuskegee National Forest that was part of William Bartram's route through Alabama became the first designated US Forest Service Trail in the nation. Pictured (from left) at the trail's dedication are Elaine Thomas with Tuskegee Institute (now Tuskegee University); AEQA Executive Vice President Martha McInnis; Tuskegee Mayor Johnny Ford; G. J. Koellsted, manager of the Auburn University Theatre who depicted Bartram during the event; Congressman Bill Nichols, who was instrumental in achieving the trail designation; an unidentified member of the Prattville YMCA "Indian dancers" troop that gave a presentation at the event; and Arthur Woody, state Forest Service supervisor with the US Department of Agriculture. (Courtesy of the AEQA.)

Georgia, Florida, Tennessee, Alabama, Mississippi, and Louisiana— were renewing a push to commemorate Bartram's work by locating and marking his route through those states as a National Scenic Trail.

According to McInnis, garden clubs as well as other organizations in the Southeast had been leading efforts to establish such a trail for years prior to this. Thanks to those efforts, sections of the trail had been established in Alabama, including a one-mile foot trail developed by the US Forest Service with support from US Congressman Bill Nichols, which opened in Macon County's Tuskegee National Forest in 1975 and was the first US Forest Service National Recreational Trail in the nation. That same year, an eight-mile section of Alabama's Tensaw Delta was also designated by the state as the Bartram Canoe Trail.

The AEQA recognized that expanding this trail would greatly benefit Alabama by providing inexpensive, pollution-free recreational opportunities to the state's citizens as well as boosting tourism, creating jobs, and opening up opportunities for scientific and historic exploration. The association immediately began to use its connections with Governor George Wallace to further the cause.

The first step toward gaining a multi-state National Scenic Trail designation was to conduct a feasibility study, not an easy task. "At the time, different states were getting their congressional delegates to introduce legislation for each state, which meant that separate bills were constantly being put up before Congress," said McInnis.

Realizing that a multi-state, inclusive bill would have more chance of passing in Congress, the AEQA enlisted Wallace's help to bring together representatives from the eight states to work on just such a comprehensive piece of legislation. In February 1975, Wallace sent a letter drafted by the AEQA staff to each of his fellow southeastern governors calling for the formation of a Bartram Trail Interstate Commission. The letter asked those governors to send representatives from each of their states to Montgomery to discuss the possibility of establishing a regional trail and an interstate commission that could provide a coordinated course of action across state boundaries and among state and federal agencies.

Wallace put McInnis and the AEQA in charge of organizing this meeting, the first gathering of which was held November 3–4, 1975, in Montgomery. Among the ninety participants were representatives from each of the governor's offices and from each state's conservation and historic preservation departments and agencies, bicentennial commissions, conservation organizations, garden clubs, and other interested groups.

"At that point we had a united front with all of the states working toward the same goal and it was amazing how well everyone worked together," said McInnis. "This would not have taken place If Wallace had not sent that letter."

Following that meeting, the Bartram Trail Conference, a 501(c)3 not-for-profit agency, was established, holding its first gathering on June 1, 1976, in Montgomery hosted by the AEQA. Soon thereafter, through the efforts of the Conference, legislation was introduced by Congress allowing the US Department of Interior's National Park Service to conduct a feasibility study on the creation of a regional National Bartram Scenic Trail, under the auspices of the National Trails Act of 1968.

The passing of that legislation, which was the last bill in Congress before a recess, was touch-and-go. "The National Park Service was shepherding this bill though Congress," recalled McInnis, "but they were having trouble getting it on the floor, and it was the last day of the session. They called us to see if we could help."

McInnis, using her political connections yet again, contacted Alabama's US Senator James B. Allen, who was a whiz at parliamentary procedure and who got the bill to the floor in the nick of time. "About eleven p.m. on that last night, I got a call from someone in Allen's office telling me 'It just passed,'" recalled McInnis.

President Gerald Ford signed the bill in October 1976; however, that authorization did not provide funding for the study. Accordingly, during their first organizational meeting held in November

1976 in Darien, Georgia, Conference members laid out a strategy to lobby Congress for funding. Its members also elected McInnis as chairman of the Conference.

Their efforts were rewarded when President Jimmy Carter signed the authorization of funding in May 1977. By October 1977, plans for the Bartram Trail feasibility study, which would be administered through the National Park Service's Bureau of Outdoor Recreation, were announced. The Bartram Trail Conference, with McInnis at the helm, was contracted to conduct the study, which would determine Bartram's place in the history of the region and develop a plan to incorporate that history into a recreation and education plan for the states involved.

"We wanted the best person to head the study," McInnis said. The choice fell on Robert M. Peck, a writer, naturalist, and historian who was at the time special assistant to the president of the Academy of Natural Sciences of Philadelphia.

According to McInnis, Peck was ideal for this project because he was extremely familiar with Bartram's history and was well connected with other top experts who could assist in the study. Jerome Anderson of the US Department of Interior office in Atlanta was chosen as project administrator for the plan.

Over the next two years, the Bartram Trail Conference held public meetings and symposia in each of the eight states to talk about ideas while Peck, working with other experts, began marking Bartram's route and identifying and classifying Bartram sites.

In addition to the study led by Peck, the AEQA also became involved in other land and historic preservation projects in the state and region. Among these was another feasibility study to explore the possibility of developing a museum-like structure that would document Bartram's travels in Alabama.

By that time Alabama and other states had designated specific sites along segments of the Bartram Trail for public use, with others in planning stages. However, no facility existed to capture and translate Bartram's diverse heritage to the people of the region. As a solution, in 1979 the AEQA used a seven thousand dollar Alabama Bicentennial grant to hire Randal Roark, an Atlanta architect on the faculty at Georgia Tech, to conduct a study for a Bartram Heritage Interpretation Center. Roark spent nearly two years working on the study and gathering input from a wide range of players who could conceivably be involved in the creation of such a center. His report was released in March 1981.

The following year, Peck's Bartram Trail feasibility study was published. It is, according to McInnis, "to this day still one of the most complete and valuable studies ever conducted on Bartram's travels."

But the results of Peck's study were ultimately disappointing. McInnis, who had been re-elected as chairman of the Bartram Trail Conference, announced: "Officials in charge of the study concluded that the trail is not feasible at this time to warrant such a designation (as a National Scenic Trail)." No official reason was ever given for this conclusion, though McInnis suspected that the lack of federal dollars to fund such a project played a big role in the final decision.

"It was aggravating that so much effort and money had been invested in this project," she said. "The Park Service probably made the decision that it would not work, in part because they were operating on limited funds, but I've also often wondered if it was dropped because it was in the South," she added.

Sadly, none of the states involved in the effort had the money to make it happen, either, and it became evident that it was better to look at designating the trail from a historic, rather than scenic, trail perspective.

"We did not succeed in having it designated," said Nancy Callahan, who was working as the AEQA communications specialist at the time. "But even so, we made people all over the Southeast aware of Bartram and made people in Alabama aware that this naturalist from Philadelphia came down during the Revolutionary War and went through what later became seven counties in Alabama. Looking back to the day of Bartram, it was a tribute to the natural riches of Alabama that he would come here more than two hundred years ago."

The Bartram Trail was not the only focus of the AEQA's effort to preserve and protect natural areas in the state. Among its other projects was a 1978 publication, *Trails of Alabama*, which catalogued more than one hundred and fifty Alabama trails. Callahan, who developed and wrote the publication, said it was one of her proudest accomplishments. "It included trails in every county in Alabama," she said, noting that she walked many of the trails herself before writing *Trails*. It was the first such compilation of its kind in the state and was quite popular. "We sold seven thousand copies," Callahan recalled.

That same year, the AEQA also published *A Policy Guide to Issues of the Alabama Environment 1978*, a publication developed at the request of politicians, public policy makers, and ecologically conscious citizens aimed at providing information that could be used to formulate public policy. The *Policy Guide* addressed a wide array of topics that were looming for the coming decade, and using this publication as proof of the need, McInnis called for legislation to develop a complete data bank of the state's "natural riches," noting that funding for this could come from a proposed tax on companies using such natural resources as sand, gravel, coal, and gas.

Among the issues the *Policy Guide* addressed were hazardous waste, litter, water quality, energy conservation, resource recovery, wilderness preservation, and highway beautification. It also helped identify specific needs in land and historic site preservation, such as restoration of Old Cahawba in Dallas County; protection of Ala-

Figure 19. *Trails of Alabama*, a best-selling AEQA publication that catalogued more than one hundred and fifty public and private trails in the state, was researched and written by Nancy Callahan (center), the AEQA's communications specialist at the time. Pictured with Callahan are Mallieve Breeding (left) of Selma, a member of the Region 6 Environmental Quality Council, and Ann Upchurch (right), a member of the Montgomery Clean Community Committee. (Photography by Jean Martin, courtesy of the *Selma Times Journal*.)

bama's National Natural Landmarks, including the Mobile-Tensaw Delta; preservation of Alabama's islands and setting aside land on Dauphin Island for a state park; development of state trail and Wild and Scenic Rivers systems; and protection of the state's wild and endangered animals and plants.

Lady Byrd Johnson, who was chairing the National Park System Advisory Board, was encouraging the preservation of a one hundred ninety–acre tract of wetlands in Mobile and Baldwin counties. It was announced that the National Park Service would conduct a forty thousand dollar study of the land and would be using information from Peck's Bartram Trail feasibility study in its efforts.

In October 1978, the idea of reviving and preserving Old Ca-hawba was also gaining momentum with AEQA backing. Accord-ing to McInnis, the AEQA's interest in Old Cahawba came about when she and John Bloomer were invited by then-Dallas County Probate Judge Johnny Jones to tour the site and other historic sites in the area.

"It was obvious that Dallas County had a tremendous resource there," said McInnis, who worked with the Dallas County Cham-ber of Commerce to launch a restoration plan. She also helped the Chamber connect with Roark, who by then had completed the Bar-tram Interpretation Center study, and he set to work doing a similar study for Old Cahawba.

"The AEQA encouraged the restoration, but it was the Dallas County Chamber of Commerce that really took the bull by the horns at Old Cahawba," said McInnis. "We just helped get things started."

According to McInnis, the AEQA's work with trails and historic sites were examples of how they filled vacuums in Alabama's en-vironmental infrastructure, taking on things such as the Bartram Trail Conference, the trails publication, and other projects for which there was at the time no state agency or position dedicated to that that work: "It was yet another void that we filled."

10
Teaching Teachers

Because environmental education was the AEQA's top priority, McInnis was always looking for fresh, innovative educational programming opportunities, and, in 1980, she found an ideal prospect through a new employee, Mike Schrier.

Schrier had come to Alabama from Michigan six years earlier to join the faculty in the College of Education at Auburn University-Montgomery. In addition to teaching upperclassmen and graduate students at AUM, Schrier also used his background in fisheries and wildlife sciences to establish an environmental science education program at the university. The program was designed to teach K through 12 teachers about environmental issues and show them how to incorporate these topics and issues into their lesson plans and curricula.

At that time, said Schrier, the environmental movement of the 1960s had grown enough so that terms like "ecology" and "ecosystems" were part of everyday language, but many people were still intimidated by "science." Schrier believed that science would be more accessible to the public if teachers could show their students how the environment connects to their daily lives. It was, he said, "a wide open opportunity."

As he was developing this idea at AUM, Schrier heard about a program being sponsored by Union Camp Corporation—a pulp and paper company headquartered in Wayne, New Jersey—that was establishing teacher education programs in several states, including Georgia. "Our director of development at AUM heard about the Union Camp workshops under way in Statesboro, Georgia (at Georgia Southern)," recalled Schrier. Together with the university administrator, Schrier spent a couple of days at the Georgia Southern workshop that summer. They immediately recognized that a similar program would be ideal to incorporate in the environmental graduate student education program at AUM.

The following summer, AUM held its first summer Teachers Environmental Technology Institute (TETI), thanks to a grant from Union Camp that paid tuition and a stipend for up to twenty teachers to attend the two-week workshop based out of Montgomery. The format for the workshop included lectures on the AUM campus provided by experts about a wide range of environmentally related issues, as well as field trips through which participants could get hands-on training.

The program was quite successful, so much so that it was nominated for the AEQA's Environmental Quality Awards program in 1978. It also introduced Schrier to the AEQA, a connection that became very important a couple of years later when, in June 1980, Schrier was hired on to the AEQA staff to replace Frank Filgo, who left the AEQA to take a job with the Alabama Trucking Association.

When Schrier was hired, McInnis immediately recognized the potential for TETI as an AEQA program. "Her light bulbs went on and she realized AEQA could make use of this too," he said, adding they started their first AEQA TETI program in the summer of 1980.

"It was a pretty good program when I did it at AUM, but it got even better when it went to the AEQA," said Schrier. "I was instrumental in helping put it together, but because of who she (McInnis) was, it got better. Martha was a master organizer who knew people in the catacombs of the state. It's a multiplier effect."

According to Schrier, McInnis's contacts were not only extensive, they were diverse, ranging from politicians to experts on a wide variety of science, environmental, and cultural issues. For example, McInnis connected TETI with Mary Ann Neeley, who had just retired from teaching in the Montgomery public school system and was helping establish Old Alabama Town, Montgomery's historic district. As Schrier noted, Neeley's historical expertise helped show the teachers that the environment really was all around them. "Mary Ann illustrated the fact that you can have 'environment' right here in the city, too," he said.

Other speakers for the TETI program ranged from university scientists to myriad others working in environmentally related professions, including a colorful riverboat pilot from south Alabama who worked on the Mississippi River as well as the Tennessee-Tombigbee waterway. "He was a spokesman for the riverboat union, and just as folksy as he could be, a little earthy at times," recalled Schrier. "We had to ask him to clean up the language," he added with a chuckle. "He would come in and pass out to each participant Mark Twain's *Life on the Mississippi* and say to them, 'This will give you an idea of what we are doing out there.'"

It was that rich diversity of information that made the TETI program especially effective, and though the program only lasted three years under the AEQA umbrella, it continued on for several years back at AUM, stronger for having been in the AEQA fold. "We (the AEQA) became history by the fall of 1983, but before that time the program flourished," Schrier said, noting that when he left the AEQA to be an education specialist with the Civil Air Patrol, he took with him many valuable lessons from the AEQA experience.

At the time that Schrier joined the staff, the AEQA was facing a funding struggle, something that was not entirely unexpected since Fob James, who had been elected governor in 1979, was now in the governor's mansion. McInnis and her staff were unsure whether the new governor would support the AEQA or seek to take away its state funding. Initially he appeared to be supportive and even carried on the tradition of designating April as Environmental Quality Month in Alabama. In making the announcement James said, "it is most appropriate to set forth a special time to celebrate the progress our state has made in its quest for environmental quality and to assess the continuing role Alabama must play to preserve her natural resources and quality of life for all her people." He also praised the AEQA for "providing Alabamians with sound, factual information" and labeled the state's environmental education organization "the vehicle for grassroots participation in the sound environmental and economic development of Alabama."

Despite his praise, though, James omitted AEQA's one hundred seventy-five thousand dollar allocation from his 1979 education budget proposal, a crisis for the AEQA that was narrowly averted with the help of some of the association's legislative supporters.

"Gerald Dial (a longtime state senator from Lineville, Alabama) was instrumental in trying to help when Fob took us out of the budget," McInnis recalled. "I stayed down there (at the Statehouse) till about two A.M. and it got put back in. Fob was there trying to work his budget and, when it had been reinstated in the budget, I said 'Now, Governor, we got it put back in so don't you take it out.'"

Despite all the push and pull for funding, Fob James presided at the eleventh annual AEQA awards program in Montgomery on August 28, 1979, during which he addressed the AEQA budget negotiations. "I met Martha McInnis for the first time during this year's budget hearings. She is very persistent," he said.

11
Ramping Up Recycling

Recycling had been a major focus of the AEQA's work from its beginnings, but those efforts gained greater momentum when, in March 1974, the association collaborated with Alabama Public Television and other local sponsors to host a statewide recycling weekend, a "first-of-its-kind venture."

The following year, the AEQA's programs were highlighted on a national stage, as the organization was invited to present a paper at the prestigious American Association for the Advancement of Science's (AAAS) 141st annual meeting on Science and Human Environment Symposium held in New York City in January 1975. That paper, titled "Regional Environmental Quality Councils," outlined the AEQA's success in establishing a statewide environmental education program and provided advice on how other states could do the same.

The AEQA and AAAS came together again in June 1975 when the two organizations cosponsored a regional seminar in Montgomery titled "Energy Conservation: Resource Recovery and Reclamation." That seminar, which was part of the AAAS's Public Un-

Figure 20. Recycling was a relatively new concept in the 1970s as the AEQA began to rally support for organized recycling campaigns. (Courtesy of the AEQA.)

derstanding of Science program, focused on the technology of a resource recovery program as well as the challenges and potentials of such programs. Following that meeting, the AEQA called for the formation of a governmental task force to study Alabama's options for dealing with solid waste management.

At the time, especially in light of the national energy crisis, a great deal of emphasis was being placed on ways to conserve energy. Resource recovery through recycling fit beautifully into that effort, but it also was of special interest in Alabama because the EPA and then the state had just instituted new sanitary landfill regulations that greatly increased the cost of maintaining and building local landfills.

According to Mike Forster, who worked with the Alabama Energy Office—an agency within the Alabama Department of Economic and Community Development—up until that time, Alabama had more than one hundred sanitary landfills that took household garbage. Under the new rules, which required two hundred fifty thousand dollars or more of investment to get landfills up to code, most communities could not afford to build or run them.

"We went from at least one landfill in each county to twenty-eight or twenty-nine in the whole state," said Forster. That left communities trying to figure out what to do with their garbage, and for many the only answer was to ship it to a more distant landfill. However, many small communities were looking for ways to reduce the amount of garbage they had to ship. Reducing the volume of trash by taking out recyclables, grass clippings, and other reusable items was one answer.

For Forster, though, it all had to tie back to energy savings. His agency had been born out of the 1973–74 US oil crisis, which began when the members of the Organization of Arab Petroleum Exporting Countries (OAPEC, consisting of the Arab members of the OPEC plus Egypt, Syria, and Tunisia) proclaimed an oil embargo against the United States. Because of that embargo, along with another oil crisis that erupted in the late 1970s when the Shah of Iran was deposed, the US Department of Energy developed a number of energy conservation programs that provided funds to states to work with an array of clients such as nonprofits, municipalities, schools, hospitals, and other groups and organizations to start or expand energy conservation measures.

According to Forster, the programs focused on myriad issues and needs, such as energy-proofing older public buildings, helping cities sequence signal lights to improve motorists' fuel efficiencies, and encouraging car pooling, ride sharing, and mass transit. Recycling, initially, was not part of their funding focus, but Forster saw that a tremendous amount of energy savings could be realized by recycling plastics, paper, glass, metal, and many other materials.

"I felt strongly about it, but I did not know how to convince DOE to use some of the funds they were providing to Alabama to support solid waste recycling," he said. The regional DOE office in Atlanta told Forster that, if he could document energy savings in BTUs (British thermal units, which they used as the common denominator for energy measurement), they would consider funding some recycling projects.

Forster also recognized that recycling could be an economic boost, something the paper industry and other industries had already discovered and were putting into practice by using recycled materials in their products. "These people weren't involved in recycling because they were tree huggers," he said. "They were relying on waste for their livelihood." Among the top users of recycled materials were Alabama's many paper mills, which relied so heavily on recycled materials that they brought bales of paper and cardboard into Alabama mills from all over the country. "Why not use paper from right here in Alabama? It just made sense," said Forster.

As he was working to find a way to help fund start-ups or support existing recycling efforts with DOE money, Forster found the AEQA. "I stumbled upon Martha at one of the AEQA's meetings or conferences and asked her, 'Do you have any resources or contacts with the metals, plastic, glass, and paper people about their energy savings?'"

Not only did the AEQA have those contacts, it was able to help Forster identify nonprofit groups that were involved with recycling efforts. Equally important, the association helped Forster make a strong case for funding recycling programs. "Martha had a calculation method that could convert tons, pounds, and gallons of recycled products into BTUs," he said. McInnis gladly shared those figures with Forster, who sent them on to the DOE. "The numbers were the rationale, justification, and backup I needed."

The AEQA also helped establish the Alabama Recycling Coalition, a nonprofit that brought together all the city, county, and nonprofit recycling coordinators with the industry representatives, waste haulers, end users, Alabama Power, and many others to further the recycling effort.

The association also established the Southeast Recycling Database, which was patterned after the Chicago Board of Trade's Commodity Exchange and designed to be a marketplace for waste materials that still had value in product manufacturing. The database, which later became known as the Recyclers Market Exchange, matched sources of waste material with potential buyers, thus facilitating economic gains while keeping waste materials out of landfills.

In 1978, the EPA awarded a contract to the AEQA to establish a market database for recycling businesses, in large part because the organization had been putting together lists of recycling companies for several years, making it a natural fit for the grant.

From all this recycling work also sprang the Southeastern Recycling Conference, an event that brought buyers and sellers of recycled materials together in one location. The conference, which still goes on today, was a huge success and eventually became an international meeting. But its beginnings required a great deal of collaboration.

Hazel Mobley, a longtime glass consultant and pioneer in the glass recycling industry, was one of the AEQA's early collaborators on the development of recycling markets and the conference. Mobley initially became involved in recycling because, she said, "I happened to be sitting in the right spot at the right time." She was work-

Figure 21. In 1980, leaders of the Beloit Community in Dallas County, who had embraced recycling with zeal, were big winners at the annual AEQA awards luncheon. Pictured here is Rosa Whitt, a member of the Beloit Community Organization, Inc., who also penned a poem of thanks to the AEQA. (Courtesy of the AEQA.)

ing for Owens Illinois, at the time the world's largest glass plant, and the company decided they had to put some effort into recycling. "I was there in sales at that time and they just said, 'Let's just do something token' (about recycling). But we did not do 'token,'" Mobley said. "Once I got involved, we did the whole thing."

However, getting people and businesses to embrace recycling did take some work. "Until that time, it was not part of everyday life," said Mobley, "especially in the South and most especially in Alabama. But it was a time when recycling needed to be done. When the focus was put in place, people were interested in doing it," she added.

Mobley recalled that one of the reasons she and others were so passionate about this cause was the journey of *Mobro 4000*—dubbed the "Gar-barge" by the media—a barge that gained infamy in 1987 for hauling the same load of trash along the east coast of North America from New York to Belize and back until a way was finally found to dispose of the garbage. She learned about AEQA's recycling efforts through *EnviroSouth* magazine, which she described as being "like the gospel" for the recycling sector and beyond. After reading in its pages that the AEQA was looking for someone to work on glass recycling, Mobley volunteered to help.

"We would go to other conferences and we would talk about doing something with recycling, but we never did," said Mobley. Not until, that is, the AEQA got involved in recycling. "It was truly Martha's vision," said Mobley, adding that, without the AEQA's help and efforts "none of us would have been as good as we were in our positions."

Mobley went on to say that the AEQA-led Southeastern Recycling Conference and the coalition of people that it developed to promote and facilitate recycling was "the greatest thing for the Southeast that we ever had happen."

One of the biggest challenges when the Southeastern Recycling Conference began was to find funding for the activities. Many companies and organizations were exceptionally helpful, providing financial and in-kind support. Among them were the Blount Foundation, Owens Brockway, Waste Management, Southeast Paper Manufacturing, Newark Paper Group, and the Alabama Power Foundation.

Though much progress was being made within the recycling business sector, work was also under way back at the grassroots level, such as in Beloit, an African-American community in west Alabama. In 1980, Beloit residents, led by Finis Harris, won first place in the AEQA's civic-service club category for their efforts, which included opening the first recycling center in their area and collecting glass, scrap tin, and paper for reuse after processing. The group was also helping support the effort to save Old Cahawba, their geographic neighbor, and had taken the lead in "Cahawba Day" activities the previous May as well as participating in the annual Selma-Dallas County Rubbish Round-Up and serving on the local Beautification Council.

Harris, along with Beloit's Activities Chairperson Rosa Whitt and Beloit Community Secretary Annie Williams, accepted the award at that year's AEQA awards luncheon and, following the event, sent a poem of thanks to the AEQA and McInnis. That poem, written by Whitt, read:

AEQA . . .
Four letters . . . words that to us mean so much . . .
Time does not permit my mentioning
All of the things on which they touch.
But just to show our appreciation
For the services on us endowed
We pause to say "Thank You!"
With hearts and heads humbly bowed.

We are proud to make our environment cleaner.
Proud to make our communities safer and more sightly to see
But to also have some coins to pocket
Made the venture more than just a spree.

We learned to save some of almost everything
And, where shown how to recycle them—where and when,
Things that we once threw away or discarded
We now use over and over again!

Figure 22. The AEQA's recycling efforts soon paid off, as the economic benefits of recycling began to be recognized by various industries. (Courtesy of the AEQA.)

To us this had helped inflation,
Our health has greatly improved
And those ugly dump piles that once were eyesores
From our community have been removed.

But the best thing that AEQA has done for us
Was when we heard the sound,
"Beloit, you have won a First Place Honor,
For your Award—Come on Down!"

Figure 23. Glass was a major focus of the Beloit Community's recycling program. Pictured (from left) are Beloit Community Organization members Annie Williams, Myrtlene Williams, Finis Harris, Odessa Pernell, and Rosa Whitt. Harris developed a portable glass-crushing machine, which he brought to Montgomery in 1980 to demonstrate to national glass recycling companies. (Courtesy of the AEQA.)

The Beloit folks also taught some things to the industry folks. Finis Harris had developed a special glass crusher that they used in Beloit. He hauled it all the way to Montgomery to show it to representatives of Owens Brockway, who incorporated some of Harris's ideas into their plants.

All of the AEQA's efforts to support recycling were making a difference. A 1980 AEQA survey of forty-three Alabama recycling operations in Alabama showed that aluminum recycling increased 1,900 percent over 1979 figures. More than 25,000 tons of aluminum were recycled along with 152,407.03 tons of miscellaneous scrap metal, an 850 percent rise; 82,093 tons of paper in 1980, a 10.7 percent increase, and 2,414 tons of glass, or a 7.5 percent increase.

In July 1982, the AEQA's recycling program was ranked first among ten programs by the Alabama Department of Energy. And as further proof of the growing awareness about recycling, a short blurb from the August 1, 1979, issue of the *Mobile Press* noted that recycling was even under way in the Statehouse:

> Rep Ann Bedsole picked up on something Clerk of the House John Pemberton has been doing for some time—and that is getting rid of the mass of paper accumulated in one session.
>
> Mrs. Bedsole asked all the House members to collect their waste paper—unapproved bills and so forth—and put it in containers to be taken to a Montgomery paper mill where it would be recycled.
>
> In the Senate, McDowell Lee, Clerk of the Senate, was doing the same thing through the coordination tactics of Miss Martha McInnis, director of the Alabama Environmental Quality Association.
>
> So . . . now you know what happens to all those bills which don't make it.

12
Developing PRIDE

In 1979, during the annual awards luncheon in Montgomery, the AEQA unveiled a new initiative—Project PRIDE, a community improvement program designed to help towns and cities prepare for the future while protecting the environment through planned sustainable growth and development. When the program was officially announced, PRIDE (an acronym for Private Revitalization in Developing the Environment) was described as "a structured community improvement program whose flexibility makes it adaptable to any size community in the state."

The premise behind PRIDE was similar to the rationale driving other community certification programs, explained McInnis. "At the time, there were already designations such as the Prepared Cities Program sponsored by the Alabama Development Office, and PRIDE played off those." As with the Prepared Cities Program, communities received PRIDE certification once they met certain criteria. "When you came into town and saw 'PRIDE certified' on the

Kiwanis or Civitan signs, it could help a community sell itself. That was the ultimate objective," McInnis said.

The PRIDE program was developed with the help of community and regional planners, experts at Auburn University and the University of Alabama-Birmingham, and representatives from chambers of commerce and other community development and leadership groups.

PRIDE worked by offering "planning-for-progress modules" that helped local leaders and citizens identify the strengths and weaknesses of their community and work to improve local conditions. The assessment list included four primary areas: personal growth (schools, cultural resources, community involvement, etc.); economy (jobs, businesses and industries, tourism potential, etc.); community facilities and services (public spaces, public services, housing, and the like); and environmental quality (recreational areas, public lands, waste control, water quality, etc.).

But it also worked to return control and planning to the local level. When announcing the launch of PRIDE in 1979, McInnis said, "Project PRIDE will return decision making to where it belongs, the local level." She went on to say, "The government has said 'Look what I can do for you!' for so long that today's society now expects the government to do everything for us. The AEQA believes it is time to return local decision-making to local citizens, to let local citizens evaluate their communities, and to let local citizens plan for orderly growth and prosperity.

"As one of the nation's fastest growing areas, it is imperative that Alabama prepare for growth and development," she added. "We are challenged to avoid the problems that urbanization and industrial development have brought to many parts of the country."

Mike Schrier, working in 1980 as AEQA program coordinator, helped promote PRIDE across the state and believed PRIDE had

Figure 24. Project PRIDE, a community certification program established by the AEQA, began taking off in the 1980s. Pictured (from left) installing PRIDE signs in Talladega are AEQA Executive Vice President Martha McInnis; Gay Langley, one of the original rural cleanup volunteers who became a leader in her community and on the state Alabama Farm Bureau Federation board; AEQA Program Development Director Mike Schrier; and Talladega Chamber of Commerce Director Lee Hoffman. (Photograph by Mike Riley, *Talladega Daily Home*; used with permission.)

great potential to help communities. "PRIDE was all about instilling pride in community," he said, noting that before the AEQA closed its doors in 1983, a number of communities across the state had become PRIDE certified.

"The goal that PRIDE represented was good, we just did not have the hosses (staff) to carry it off," he said. "The AEQA did one form or another of work in all sixty-seven counties. But for a staff of our size to try to impact sixty-seven counties was tough. Even Superman would have wilted under that one." In his view, "There was a future if the money and resources had been there. But we just couldn't carry the whole ball."

Still, Schrier believes the spirit of PRIDE has been carried on through similar programs, such as the Alabama Treasure Forest program. "The effect went on for years. It had an impact. That was the forte of Martha," he said. "She was a visionary, a pacesetter, a trendsetter."

For all its promise, though, PRIDE may also have been one of the reasons that the AEQA became a bigger target for politicians, who may well have seen PRIDE as a program that would fully solidify the AEQA's existence and presence. "They were afraid of that," said McInnis. "It was probably the best thing we ever came up with," she recalled, "and it was really ready to blossom. It would have been wonderful to see it accepted."

13
Saving Parker Island

In the fall of 1980 a new land and heritage preservation effort began when, in October, it was announced that foreign investors were poised to buy Parker Island, a roughly two thousand–acre site located at the confluence of the Coosa and Tallapoosa rivers near Fort Toulouse and home to a number of ancient Native American mounds.

The island was privately owned by a group of Florida-based partners who had purchased the land in 1948 but wanted to sell the island and reinvest the money in farmland near Quincy, Florida. According to news reports, the partners had signed a sixty-day agreement in early September with potential buyers described as "from outside the United States," who were willing to purchase the land for $1.8 million.

When the AEQA caught wind of the sale in October 1980, the staff sprang into action, calling a press conference to announce the impending sale of the island to what was described as a British company, "reportedly financed with oil money."

From that press conference came an *Alabama Journal* article written by Nick Lackeos and titled "Toulouse Panel Seeks to Keep British Out of Area—Again." In the article, Lackeos stated: "The French built Fort Toulouse in the 1700s to keep the British out of surrounding territory, and a press conference was held today for the same reason—to keep the British out."

The conference ignited quite a response from historians and preservationists in the state, including Milo Howard, then the director of the Alabama Department of Archives and History; Mack Brooms, an archeologist with the Alabama Historical Commission; Larry Oaks, director of the Alabama Historical Commission; and Larry Haikey, tribal planner for the Creek Indian Nation East of the Mississippi.

Brooms noted that archeological finds on the island dated back to 6,000 BC, and Howard explained that the area had become an island about ninety-four years earlier following the flood of 1886, before which there had been pedestrian access to the island. The territory was rich in timber, gravel, and wildlife, said Brooms, and had been inhabited by "nomadic tribes that would come and go from one season to another until around 500 AD to 900 AD when some built towns and raised crops. Some tribes mysteriously vanished from the area at different points in history." He added that the Creeks eventually came to the area, raised crops, and thrived until white soldiers drove them out in the 1800s to make room for settlers.

In an effort to save Parker Island (sometimes called Parker's Island) and its history, the AEQA joined with the Alabama Historical Commission, the Alabama Department of Conservation and Natural Resources, and the Creek Indian Nation to wage a campaign aimed at raising the $1.8 million needed to buy the island before the sale was finalized.

The AEQA not only wanted to preserve the land but also saw the island as a way to make the Bartram Heritage Interpretation Center, which was being developed at the time by Randal Roark, a reality. "The foreign money might use the island as a source of gravel and timber," McInnis was quoted in news reports as saying. "We want to develop it as part of a cultural complex that would serve the people as a source of culture and education."

McInnis felt the island could become part of a complex featuring Fort Toulouse and "Hickory Ground," the last capital of the National Council of the Creek Nation, which had recently been acquired from a private landowner by the Alabama Historical Commission and the Poarch Band of Creek Indians for historic preservation. "Those three resources linked together would form an interpretive system of regional and national significance and would be a major attraction of the state of Alabama," she said.

Milo Howard agreed with McInnis, saying that Parker Island was "a treasure house with a wealth of historical material." He added that allowing it to be bought by strangers "is really something for the state to be alarmed about."

Though there was plenty of concern about the sale, the campaign also brought about some humorous needling from the media. An October 26, 1980, *Montgomery Advertiser* editorial by Lackeos that ran shortly after the AEQA press conference stated: "Within a few short weeks, Wetumpka has escaped Cubans, Russians, and now, the British are hammering at the gates." Namely, "The city council had dealt with an imaginary encampment of Cubans along the riverbank; a solemn County Commission established a succession of power in case a Russian invasion brought an untimely end to Probate Judge Ed Enslen. A press conference Wednesday warned of the Red Coats."

Lackeos went on to note that, during the AEQA-sponsored press conference announcing concerns about the island's sale, "For hunters and hikers and campers, Jimmy Shaw spoke up for the island, saying there are 'three hundred fifty thousand licensed hunters in

Alabama,' and that if each contributed five dollars, the association would have enough money to buy the island." Lackeos concluded that "some reporters came away with an impression of kinship between an island in Wetumpka and a bridge to Brooklyn."

Another editorial in the *Montgomery Advertiser* on October 23, 1980, titled "One If by Land," also addressed the controversy by stating:

> It isn't at all clear, however, what the British would do to it that we wouldn't. Of all the world's exploiters, they know about islands.
>
> That area of the river was most recently in the news as sheltering an encampment of three hundred Cubans about which the Wetumpka City Council was warned. They were never found, but nobody searched the island.
>
> Someone should notify London.

As a plan to save the island was formulated, Archie Hooper, assistant director of the Alabama Department of Conservation and Natural Resources, noted that the state could use federal funds as fifty–fifty matches with counties and cities to buy land such as this, but he added, "The backlog of requests already is large. Also, we must restore Gulf State Park, which was devastated by Hurricane Frederick and we have other state parks needing funds."

Hooper went on to caution that the project could cost much more than the $1.8 million purchase price, saying, "During bad floods, the island—which is where the Coosa and Tallapoosa rivers converge to make the Alabama River—has been entirely underwater. Any meaningful development would have to include flood prevention."

Though the island's owners were open to the idea of the state buying and preserving the island, they also were anxious to sell the land so that they could plan farming operations for next year. And, it turned out, more than one buyer was interested. "The plot thickened in a story of historic Parker Island near Fort Toulouse in Elmore County with the filing of a purchase agreement between owners and Thomson Forestry Inc., identified as a Delaware corporation," said an October 31, 1980, article in the *Montgomery Advertiser*.

According to the article, paperwork filed in Elmore County Probate Court listed the purchase price at $1.35 million and noted that the price quoted by the owners for the state to buy it was $1.8 million.

As the sale closing date drew near, a November 3, 1980, letter in the *Montgomery Advertiser* by Montgomery archeologist David W. Chase highlighted the need for archeological evaluation and preservation of such treasures as Parker Island, stating: "Parker Island must not be added to the list of Alabama's archeological casualties. If somehow we could tune into voices from the 21st century, we might hear someone say 'Why didn't somebody do something about it?'"

Whether it was the hue and cry against the sale or just economics, the sale did not go through in 1980, which furthered the idea of selling the island to the state. However, those plans did not look promising, in part because the state had no funds to buy it and also because officials felt it was not feasible to develop the area into a viable state park.

John McMillan, then the Department of Conservation and Natural Resources director, did state, however, that he wanted the archeological treasures to be preserved and would seek help from the Nature Conservancy. And others joined the call to save the island, including Lindy Martin, chief executive of the Society for the Preservation of American Indian Culture, who characterized Parker Island as "a very important chapter in Alabama Indian history" that he hoped to see turned into a seat for the study of Indian culture.

Support also grew in the community, including a concerted grassroots campaign led by schoolchildren at Maxwell Air Force Base

Elementary School in Montgomery, who took to wearing "Ask Me About Parker's Island" T-shirts and soliciting donations for the AE-QA's Parker Island Fund. The students also set about writing their congressional representatives, state and local officials, the Environmental Defense Fund, and other elementary schools across the state trying to rally support for the island. In addition, they began collecting aluminum cans and paper to sell to recycling centers, with plans to use the money toward the Parker Island purchase.

An article by Staff Sergeant Bob Sims in the *Montgomery Dispatch* said that the students "are growing restless. One fifth-grader commented to an adult, 'You all need to stop talking, and start doing.'" Further, the September 17, 1981, issue of the *Columbus Enquirer* featured the children's drawings and published a poem by student Melissa Smith:

Parker's Island
Oh, Parker's Island has a way
Of telling us history in the USA
So go to Parker's Island,
Go there today.
And you'll have fun all the way.

We're number 1,
Not number 2,
We're going to buy it,
How about you?

As the year wore on, the AEQA also got help from wildlife artist Larry Martin. "Larry was so interested in the wildlife part of the island, and he offered to do a piece of art and sell prints of it to raise money," said McInnis.

Despite all these efforts, though, the island was never purchased

Figure 25. Governor Fob James (seated) tried unsuccessfully to eliminate the AEQA's funding from the state budget during his tenure but ultimately supported the AEQA's work in communities. He is pictured here signing a Governor's Proclamation designating April as Environmental Quality Month in 1981. Also pictured (from left) are Rosa Whitt of the Beloit Community, Virginia Bradshaw of Alex City's RSVP program, Mr. and Mrs. Robert Bynum of the Blount County PRIDE program, Annie Williams of the Beloit Community, Billy Simmons of the Demopolis PRIDE program, AEQA Executive Vice President Martha McInnis, AEQA Program Development Director Mike Schrier, AEQA Marketing Director John Coleman, Joshua Williams of the Beloit Community, and Harlan Shaw and Bud Porch of the Alex City RSVP program. (Courtesy of the AEQA.)

as a public site, but instead sold to a more local buyer who used it for a hunting preserve.

"We just ran out of steam on trying to protect it," said McInnis, though she still believes locating a Bartram Interpretation Center there or elsewhere in the area has great potential.

14
Doors Close, Legacies Continue

"One of the most imaginative environmental groups in the country." These were the words that David Mathews, president of the Kettering Foundation in Ohio, used to describe the AEQA when he delivered the keynote address at the association's fifteenth annual awards luncheon in June 1983.

Mathews could speak those words from a position of experience. The former president of the University of Alabama and head of the US Office of Health, Education, and Welfare had worked with McInnis and her organization before joining Kettering and had witnessed the AEQA's progress firsthand. He had seen it grow from an association eagerly tackling Alabama's solid waste cleanup problems to a regional leader on myriad environmental fronts—from helping establish the Bartram Trail Conference to teaching teachers to empowering local communities through recycling and economic and community development programs and much more.

Yes, the association's list of accomplishments was long and imaginative, and it held great promise for future progress. But a few short

Figure 26. Artist Larry Martin of Anniston helped in the AEQA's effort to save Parker Island—a tiny island rich in natural resources and cultural history located at the confluence of the Alabama and Tallapoosa rivers near Fort Toulouse— by creating this original work of art. This piece was reproduced into numbered prints that were sold to raise money toward the purchase of the island as a historical site and possibly as home to a Bartram Trail Interpretation Center. (Courtesy of Larry Martin and Wren's Nest, Inc.)

months after Mathews gave that speech, that promise fell victim to budget cuts and funding shortfalls.

Throughout its existence, the AEQA had relied on one primary and politically precarious source of funding—state dollars that were awarded at the discretion of the Alabama Legislature. As the 1980s ushered in a new era of legislative and political priorities and as the state began to develop its own internal divisions and programs that could address environmental issues, support for continued funding of the AEQA had dwindled. The state budget passed by the Alabama Legislature in 1983 reflected this shift in priorities by eliminating all state funding for the AEQA, and by October of that year the association's doors were closed.

Though the AEQA was no more, McInnis did continue working on environmental issues for many subsequent years, first as president of EnviroSouth, Inc., and later as chief of the Science, Technology, and Energy Division of Alabama's Department of Economic and Community Affairs. And though she laments the loss of the AEQA, McInnis also knows the organization's impact in the state and region was profound, a belief echoed by former Alabama Governor Albert Brewer, who had worked with McInnis and the AEQA during his gubernatorial term from 1968 to 1971.

"I look back on those early years of the AEQA and the environmental movement and see the results today," he said, noting that the AEQA and other groups were navigating a difficult, but vital path. "At the time, industries were saying 'If you make us do this, we have to close down.' Environmental groups were saying 'If we don't do this, we will have all sorts of other health problems.' It was a difficult and complicated issue. I am sure there were some industries that went out of business because the cost to clean up the environment was too great to continue profitably, but that is the price you pay." Brewer continued, "At what point do you take out the price of things that have a negative impact on human life? If nothing had been done back then, the situation was going to simply get worse."

Though the AEQA was certainly not working alone in the effort to clean up Alabama, it was a primary leader in protecting and improving Alabama's environment. And though its doors may have closed in 1983, McInnis never stopped believing in the importance of the association's citizen-based, grassroots mission. She also believes that the AEQA's legacy lives on today.

According to McInnis, the AEQA-fostered Solid Waste Disposal Act of 1969, one of the first such laws in the nation, remains the foundation of modern solid waste disposal systems in Alabama and in other states across the United States. The AEQA's Alabama Environmental Education Master Plan, also among the first of its kind in the country, became a blueprint for other states, not to mention other countries, to develop similar programs.

And while recycling is a common practice today, it was a novel idea in the 1970s when the AEQA led the charge to establish recycling programs in the state and region.

"The AEQA was pivotal in developing a recycling structure in the Southeast," said Hazel Mobley, who had worked with McInnis and the AEQA to help build today's regional recycling economy. "It's profitable to recycle now, but in the early days it was an expense you had to bear," she said. Once federal subsidies for recycling began to dwindle, the incentive for many companies to recycle also waned.

Realizing that to make recycling work in the long-term it had to become profitable, Mobley and McInnis found ways to make it just that and worked with companies such as Anheuser-Busch, Miller, and Coca Cola in Georgia to help recycle their glass waste, which laid the foundation for other industries to follow.

"Today trucks are rolling every day bringing those bottles to recycling centers and none of it goes in the landfills," Mobley said. And they didn't stop with glass. They expanded to include a wide range of recyclable waste products, a concept that was embraced by industry, municipalities, and citizens alike. "For example, Coke recycles every container whether it is plastic, glass, or aluminum."

Though much more still needs to be done to further build a recycling culture, Mobley said it has a strong foundation thanks in large part to the AEQA. "People who came up learning about recycling through the AEQA and other organizations are going to do it right," she said. "And it will get better and better until there comes a day when we don't throw anything away."

McInnis believes that the AEQA's legacy can also be recycled. "I do wonder where it (the AEQA) would have been today had we not lost our funding," she said, but she also sees the association living on in many modern-day programs.

Among those are land preservation and environmental education programs, such as the Hays Nature Preserve (named for former Alabama Farm Bureau President J. D. Hays and his wife, Annie) in Owens Crossroads, Alabama, and the Bartram Trail Conference, which is still going strong some fifty years after the AEQA helped organize the first multi-state Bartram Trail coalition.

McInnis is not only pleased that the Bartram Trail Conference is such a dynamic organization today, she also believes that the Bartram Trail Feasibility Study and Bartram Heritage Interpretation Center plan that the AEQA helped develop still hold great value. "Those documents could be used today if someone will just go dig them out of the archives," she said.

She also sees many aspects of Project PRIDE, which was just taking off when the AEQA dissolved, in similar programs today, such as Tree City USA and Scenic City designations. And, McInnis believes, PRIDE's structure could well be revived and revamped to instill a fresh sense of community spirit in Alabama.

"So much of what we did is still important today," said McInnis. "I just hope that someone will take the ideas, programs, and passion that were part of the AEQA and find new ways to use them."

If that happens, McInnis said, perhaps the grassroots movement started so accidentally by Lance Tompkins many decades ago that went on to become an important chapter in Alabama's environmental history will not only be remembered but will also live on.

Index